About the author

Alex Keen runs his own publishing business. A recovered debtor, he now writes on debt-related issues.

Acknowledgements

The author and publishers would like to thank the following for their help in the preparation of this book: Matt Cornish, Teresa Fritz, Melanie Green, Ashley Holmes, Ashleye Sharpe.

Life after debt

get your finances back on track

Alex Keen

 CONSUMERS' ASSOCIATION

Which? Books are commissioned and researched by
Consumers' Association and published by
Which? Ltd, 2 Marylebone Road, London NW1 4DF
Email address: books@which.net

Distributed by The Penguin Group:
Penguin Books Ltd, 80 Strand, London WC2R 0RL

First edition July 2003

British Library Cataloguing in Publication Data
A catalogue record for this book is available from the British Library

ISBN 0 85202 953 5

For a full list of Which? books, please call 0800 252100, access our website at
www.which.net, or write to Which? Books, PO Box 44, Hertford, SG14 1SH.

Editorial and production: Joanna Bregosz, Robert Gray, Ian Robinson, Mary
Sunderland, Barbara Toft
Cover design: Sarah Harmer
Cover photograph: David Gould/getty images

Typeset by Saxon Graphics Ltd, Derby
Printed and bound in England by Clays Ltd, Bungay, Suffolk

Contents

Foreword

Debt is an issue that affects nearly all of us. Whether it's paying the mortgage or rent, a periodic utility or council tax bill, credit-card spending, a student loan, or a personal loan or overdraft, we all have financial commitments to meet that involve some element of debt.

Over the past 20 years, the amount of outstanding debt has risen dramatically through the growth in consumer credit. An ever-increasing range of credit cards, bank accounts with overdraft facilities, flexible mortgages, personal loans and so on means a vastly increased choice in how to borrow money. More recently, the introduction of so-called 'impaired credit' products offers a borrowing opportunity to those who would previously have been refused credit by the high street banks. And to persuade us just how lucky we are to have this new opportunity, the marketing of credit is now impossible to avoid, whether by newspapers, television, telephone cold calling, email, or post.

In many ways we can benefit from these developments. Borrowing more can be a perfectly sensible choice for fully informed consumers who make optimal choices in their use of credit. Taking on additional debt can even out fluctuations in income and spending and allow us to buy today what we otherwise would have to put off until tomorrow. While our grandparents' generation would be appalled at this concept, it is now a firmly established feature of our society. On the wider scale, economists generally agree that a major recent factor in avoiding a damaging recession has been the willingness of consumers to spend money that they don't actually have.

But there is a significant downside. The growth of credit also means an increase in the number of borrowers experiencing financial difficulty. Whether it is through sickness, unemployment, the birth of a new child, over-commitment or other factors, the number of people seeking help on debt issues has risen steadily. In 2001-02, Citizens Advice Bureaux (CABs) dealt with over one million new debt cases, and there has been a 47 per cent increase in consumer credit debt problems brought to bureaux over the last five years. The growth in debt advice enquiries is such that CABs have not been able to meet the demand. One consequence of this has been the growth of commercial companies looking to make a profit from helping with debt problems, whether through offers of further loans or management of existing debt.

CABs are at the sharp end of the demand for debt advice, and advisers regularly see the misery that debt problems can bring. They also know how easy it is for someone in a viable financial situation to suddenly develop a major debt problem irrespective of age, income or social background. A survey of CAB debt clients in 2002 showed that it took only a 10 per cent drop in income to change manageable credit commitments into serious debt problems, with the result that a quarter of those surveyed were receiving treatment for anxiety, stress and depression.

The key to managing a debt problem is prompt action to put the situation back on an even keel. Too often, the problem is made worse because the individual does not know the best course of action and is even sometimes steered down the wrong road by advisers who have more of an eye on their own financial well-being than on the best solution to the problem. It is therefore vital that those facing difficulties can access high-quality information and advice that is independent and impartial, of the sort this book provides.

Nick Lord
National Head of Money Issues
Citizens Advice

Introduction

Most people have debts of some sort. From an overdraft or outstanding credit-card balance, to a loan for a new car or a mortgage to buy a house, borrowing is a convenient way of adding flexibility to our incomes. The problem comes when debts get out of hand. You can no longer see a way of paying them back, monthly instalments are increasingly hard to afford, or you cannot meet even minimum repayments. Financial difficulties of this kind can build slowly – coming to a sudden crisis with a missed repayment or unpaid bill following an unexpected change in circumstances such as illness, unemployment or business failure. Personal crisis often leads to financial crisis: divorce, bereavement or a serious accident can turn manageable borrowing into unmanageable debt (see page 11 for a list of warning signs that your debts are out of control).

For some people the answer to their problems is a simple rearrangement of their financial affairs. Reduced interest charges, better budgeting and increased awareness of their situation will sometimes be enough to sort things out. A temporary crisis can be averted and their finances put on a sounder footing to avoid more serious trouble. For others, mere tinkering will not be enough. Creditors need to be informed that there are difficulties. Repayments need to be revised. Long-term readjustments and difficult decisions are called for. *Life After Debt* looks at ways of coping with this increasingly widespread problem. The book offers practical advice on dealing with debts. It explains the difference between priority debts and non-priority debts and suggests ways of negotiating with creditors to achieve a fair outcome. Where debts are overwhelming, more drastic remedies may be needed. Bankruptcy is examined in detail, both as a voluntary solution and as an unwelcome consequence. Alternatives are clearly outlined.

This book will help you to regain control of your finances – and, through them, your life. The author knows the misery debt can bring from personal experience. He also knows the relief of getting out of the red. By following his advice, you can finally deal with your debts and find financial freedom.

This book provides general guidance only. Before taking action it is advisable to seek financial and/or legal assistance by contracting one of the organisations listed on pages 14 & 29.

CHAPTER 1

Taking stock

Warning signs

The best way to deal with debt is to nip it in the bud before it gets out of control. This means not being complacent about the warning signs, which can suggest that you are heading for trouble. If you answer yes to some or all of the following questions, you should give serious thought to sorting out your finances.

- Are you always overdrawn?
- Do you repay only the minimum amount on your credit card each month?
- Does the amount you owe on your credit card go up every month?
- Do you put off paying bills until the final reminder arrives?
- Have you ever missed a repayment on your mortgage or other loan?
- Can you afford to buy things only by borrowing?

This chapter will help you to get to grips with your debts through a series of essential steps. You'll be able to assess clearly how much you owe, the scale of your outgoings and the size of your income. With this information, you will be able to make an informed decision about the best course of action to take to tackle your debt problems.

Step 1: Gather information

Collect together every record of everything that you owe, such as unpaid bills, unopened mail, credit-card statements, unpaid utility bills, letters from debt collectors, council tax bills, fines, red reminders, final reminders, final final reminders...the lot.

Step 2: Make a list

Take a fresh notepad and a pen. Write down the name of the creditor or the collection agency on the left-hand side of the page, and the total amount that you owe each creditor on the right. Do this until you have gone through all your paperwork and you have a long list of all the money that you owe on the sheet in front of you. You should also make a note of each creditor's contact details (address and telephone number) because you need to get in touch and explain that you are in difficulties.

Step 3: Order your debts

When you come to add up your debts, you should sort them into two groups – priority debts and non-priority debts. Priority debts are those which carry particularly serious consequences if they are not dealt with, such as court action or losing your home and essential services (see Chapter 3). They include:

- mortgages and other secured loans
- rent arrears
- council tax arrears
- gas arrears
- electricity arrears
- other fuel arrears

- telephone arrears (if essential – e.g. if you work from home)
- magistrates' court fine arrears
- maintenance payment arrears
- income tax arrears
- National Insurance arrears
- VAT arrears
- hire purchase arrears (for essential items – e.g. a car for work).

Non-priority debts are those where failure to pay will not result in the loss of your liberty, home or essential goods and services (although creditors may still back their demands for payment with financial and legal sanctions – see Chapter 4). They include the following:

- bank overdrafts and unsecured loans
- credit-card arrears
- store-card arrears
- catalogue arrears (including mail order)
- hire purchase arrears (non-essential goods)
- benefits overpayments.

Priority debts come first

The reason for sorting your debts into these two groups is because, as their name suggests, priority debts have a more urgent claim on available income than non-priority debts. This means that you should deal with these first, and then see how much income, if any, is left over to pay non-priority creditors. This is sometimes difficult to remember if creditors are particularly persistent or demanding but it is important to maintain the distinction between priority and other debts.

Step 4: Calculate your income and expenditure

The next stage in tackling your debts is to work out how much money is available to you each month. List all your sources of income and draw up a detailed breakdown of all your monthly spending. You can do this by following the detailed steps on the next few pages. To find out how much money is left over for paying your debts, subtract your monthly spending from your monthly income. If you are left with a minus figure (that is, your spending exceeds your income) you need to find ways of either increasing your income or cutting back on your spending. It can be difficult deciding what to give up in order to save money. If you can't do it yourself, get help in the form of a debt adviser who will be able to take a dispassionate view of what is essential and what is not.

Debt advisers

This book cannot give more than general solutions. For personal advice tailored to your circumstances, and assistance in drawing up a financial statement and initiating negotiations with your creditors, you may want to consider enlisting the help of a debt adviser by contacting the Citizens Advice Bureau (CAB)*, a Money Advice Centre*, the Consumer Credit Counselling Service* or the National Debtline*. Getting outside help not only shows your creditors that you are serious about solving your problems, but will ensure that you get advice about any state benefits and tax allowances to which you may be entitled (see Chapter 9).

Your budget

Working out a budget is essential if you are to take control of your money. It will help you identify any changes you need to make to your spending patterns and enable you to draw up a realistic financial statement to show to your creditors.

Making a list

The first step in drawing up a budget is to make a list of everything on which you spend money. Writing this down helps to focus your mind and provides you with a permanent record you won't forget. Rather than drawing up one long list, it can be helpful to break it down into different elements, such as:

- household costs
- living expenses
- travel
- car
- personal spending
- leisure
- Christmas and birthdays
- savings
- children
- financial costs (including credit-card repayments)
- cash spending.

Establishing priorities

You should also divide your spending into two categories:

- **essential**, which covers the unavoidable and the necessary, such as your rent or mortgage, your bills, season ticket for getting to work, food, life insurance and so on
- **desirable**, which covers spending that is not *strictly* necessary (and at a push, you could do without) but which you regard as contributing to your wellbeing, such as non-work clothes, CDs and meals out.

Collecting data

The next stage is to collect financial data for your list. In most cases, this will be a combination of actual past spending and educated guesses at future spending.

If you can lay your hands on a year's worth of bank statements, cheque-book stubs, credit-card and store-card statements and other household bills, you already have a lot of the data you need to provide a detailed breakdown of your finances. If your records are less comprehensive, you may still be able to get a reasonable idea of where your money goes from your bank statements and credit-card bills.

If you do not have any records or if you are drawing up a budget to see if you can afford something in particular, you will have to estimate the figures, to give their monthly cost.

Entering the figures

Once you have collected all your data together, you can start to enter figures against the items on your list. These should be in the form of monthly totals. For some items, such as your rent or monthly mortgage, this will be straightforward. Irregular spending on items such as clothes, holidays, quarterly bills and so on, requires you to estimate how much you spend each year and then divide this figure by 12. In this way you can arrive at a monthly sum for every item (see example, opposite).

Using software

If you have a computer and spreadsheet software, you will save a lot of time if you enter your figures on a spreadsheet. This will also help if you need to adjust the figures or if you want to do 'what if?' calculations to see the effect of making various changes to your budget.

Example of part of a budget breakdown		
	Essential spending	**Desirable spending**
Household	**Monthly**	**Monthly**
Mortgage	£250	
Loan repayments	£200	
Credit-card interest charges	£50	
Council tax	£75	
Water	£17	
Electricity	£27	
Gas	£20	
Telephone	£25	
Buildings insurance	£32	
Contents insurance	£23	
Boiler service	£5	
Decorating		£50
Gardening		£25
Things for house		£20
Supermarket	£200	
TV licence	£10	
Sub-total	**£934**	**£95**
Personal		
Work clothes	£50	
Other clothes		£50
Going out		£200
CDs		£15
Books		£15

Example of part of a budget breakdown *continued*

	Essential spending	Desirable spending
	Monthly	Monthly
Gym		£33
Holidays/savings		£100
Sub-total	**£50**	**£413**
Cash spending		
Video rental		£12
Newspapers		£15
Magazines		£10
Drinks		£60
Dry cleaning	£10	
Miscellaneous		£20
Sub-total	**£10**	**£117**

Once you have entered all the figures, add up your total essential spending and your total desirable spending. This has the effect of smoothing your spending over the year to give you an average monthly spending figure for each of the two categories. These can then be entered in the 'Personal budget calculator', opposite.

Working out your average monthly income
Once you have worked out your average monthly spending, you need to work out your average monthly income. To do this:

- add up all sources of regular monthly income
- If you are paid weekly or you get other weekly income (such as child benefit or state pension), multiply the weekly amount by four.

● calculate a monthly average for any irregular income you receive, together with lump sums you withdraw from savings, by adding up an annual total and dividing this by 12.

The total of all these figures is your average monthly income, which you should enter in the 'Personal budget calculator', below.

Personal budget calculator	
Enter your average monthly income	A
Enter your average monthly spend on essentials	B
Subtract B from A and enter the result at C	C
The figure at C is what you have left to spend on desirables	
Enter your average monthly spend on desirables	D
Subtract D from C and enter the result at E	E

If your total at C is zero or negative (and you can't cut down on spending) you need to negotiate with your creditors in order to reduce your monthly repayments to a level you can afford to meet. See Chapters 3 and 4 for strategies you might adopt.

The ultimate aim of budgeting is to balance your income and expenditure. Failure to do this will lead to increasing indebtedness as you have to borrow more and more to make up for the fact that your spending exceeds your income. There are several ways to accomplish equilibrium – mainly by *decreasing* your expenditure or *increasing* your income. The following actions can help you improve your position:

● cutting back spending on inessentials
● working out a monthly budget for your essential bills
● checking that your overdraft is authorised and that you are not paying over the odds for it
● transferring all your credit-card debts to a lower-charging card

- diverting any savings you may have towards paying off your debts
- finding a cheaper way to borrow for your other loans – but be wary of transferring loans which carry a penalty for early repayment
- ensuring that you keep up repayments on your mortgage and other existing loans
- paying off the most expensive of the debts that you can clear first.

Re-mortgaging

One way to reduce your outgoings is to cut the cost of your borrowing. If you are a home-owner, and have some equity in your property, you might be able to do this by re-mortgaging.

By simply switching to a different mortgage provider, you may be able to obtain a lower rate of interest. You might also be able to replace expensive borrowing with a loan secured on your property at a much lower rate of interest. This may bring your monthly repayments down to a manageable level.

Although re-mortgaging can be an attractive option, there are several points you need to bear in mind:

1. Failing to keep up repayments on your mortgage means that your house could be repossessed. Unsecured borrowing doesn't carry this risk.

2. Always check whether you will be charged an early repayment charge (or redemption penalty) if you change to another mortgage, and find out what fees (such as solicitor's and valuation fees) you will be charged. These costs may wipe out any benefit to getting a lower rate.

3. You will only make a significant reduction in your outgoings if you change substantial high-interest borrowings to a lower rate.

4. Only re-mortgage with a licensed mortgage provider.

Step 5: Prepare a financial statement

Drawing up a financial statement not only helps you to plan but it will also show your creditors what your financial position is and how much money is available for repaying your debts. If your creditors can see that you do not have money available to repay them in full, they may realise that it is not worth taking you to court to recover the money. A financial statement can also help persuade creditors to freeze interest and to accept token payments while you concentrate on repaying your priority debts.

The example financial statement below is in two parts: the first lists your income and outgoings and shows how much you have available for repaying your debts each month; the second shows your total debts and the amount you can repay each month.

Example of a financial statement	
Name	
Address	
Income	**Monthly amount**
After-tax salary	
Partner's after-tax salary (if jointly liable for debts)	
State benefits and tax credits	
Other income (including any maintenance payments you receive)	
Total income	

Example of a financial statement *continued*

	Monthly amount
Outgoings	
Rent/mortgage	
Mortgage endowment policy	
Second mortgage/secured loans	
Council tax	
Ground rent/service charge	
Life insurance	
House insurance (buildings and contents)	
Water	
Gas	
Electricity	
Other fuel	
Telephone	
Housekeeping	
TV rental/licence	
Travelling expenses	
School meals/meals at work	
Clothing	
Prescriptions	
Court fines	
Maintenance payments you are required to make	
Childminding	
Other	
Total outgoings	

Money available for paying debts (total income less total outgoings)		£
Priority debts	**Total amount owed**	**Monthly offer of repayment**
Mortgage/rent arrears		
Second mortgage/secured loan arrears		
Council tax arrears		
Money owed for gas		
Money owed for electricity		
Court fines outstanding		
Maintenance arrears		
Other (e.g. HP essential goods)		
National Insurance		
Income tax		
Total monthly repayment of priority debts		£
Monthly amount available for other creditors (money available for repaying debts less total monthly repayment of priority debts)		£X
Non-priority debts	**Total amount owed**	**Monthly offer of repayment ***
ABC Finance		
XYZ Finance		
Visa card		
MasterCard		
Flexible friend		
Flexible foe		
Great White Collection Co.		
Catalogue A		
Raining Stones Solicitors		
Hire purchase Co (non-essential goods)		
Total	**£Y**	**£***

*To calculate this, divide the total amount owed to each creditor by the total non-priority debts (Y) and multiply by the monthly amount available for other creditors (X)

Negotiating with your creditors

Once you have drawn up a financial statement you will be in
a position to negotiate a realistic repayment plan with your
creditors, concentrating on your priority debts first (see
Chapters 3 and 4). A copy of your financial statement should
be sent with any offer of repayment to demonstrate that,
given your financial circumstances, it is a reasonable amount,
however small it may appear.

CHAPTER 2

Contacting creditors

Once you have taken stock of your debts, the first thing you
should do is contact your creditors – that is, all the organisations you owe money to (including the gas, electricity, water
and telephone companies). You can do this on your own, or
with the help of a debt adviser (see pages 28–9). The earlier
you write to your creditors explaining that you are in
financial difficulty, the more flexible and helpful they are
likely to be. If you have already started to receive reminders
and/or final demands, do not ignore them – get in touch
with the company as soon as possible to explain your situation. Your creditors may charge you some of the costs they
incur in chasing arrears, so you risk exacerbating the
problem by doing nothing. You are also more likely to face
court action (see Chapter 7).

Negotiating

To most people in serious debt, the very thought of asking
their creditors to agree to freeze interest, lower their
monthly payment or write off a significant part of it can be
extremely daunting. It may surprise you to learn that there
are many useful tips and strategies that you can employ in
your negotiations with your creditors.

If you are being pressurised by creditors, who are issuing
threatening letters and making phone calls demanding
money, it is easy to cave in to their demands and offer them

everything that they are asking for – even if you have no way of following through with your promises. Do not be bullied into doing so. The first step in the process of negotiation begins with writing a letter to the creditor setting out your position and making promises you can keep.

Writing an effective letter

When you write to your creditors, always include the creditor's name and address, your name and address (and your partner's name if you both signed a joint credit agreement) and your account number. If a creditor has already written to you concerning non-payment, include the creditor's reference number. Attach a copy of your financial statement to show why you cannot pay or to support an offer of reduced payment.

If you have no money with which to make payment, or you are offering only a token sum – for example, you can pay only £1 a month – you should:

- give reasons as to why you cannot afford to make the monthly repayment – e.g. you have just lost your job, split up with a partner or had an unexpected fall in income or increase in outgoings
- refer to your budget statement to illustrate why you cannot afford repayment
- explain what you would like the creditor to do – e.g. freeze interest and accept no payments for the next six months, or freeze interest and accept only a token payment
- ask the creditor to send you a paying-in book or standing order form (if you are making an offer of payment).

If you are offering to repay your debt at a reduced amount each month (as calculated in your financial statement in Chapter 1), also explain:

- that this is what you would like to do
- how you have calculated the reduced amount
- that you have worked it out on a 'pro-rata basis'
- that you have treated all your creditors in the same way.

Don't be tempted to offer more than you think that you can comfortably pay. Your creditor may well agree to reschedule repayments (accept a smaller amount each month, paid over a longer period) or even settle for a much lower amount than you owe if it thinks that your offer is the best that it is likely to get.

Further communication

Once they have read your letter, most creditors will be anxious to get in touch with you to discuss your situation and decide whether or not you have the means to pay them back. It can be very stressful to negotiate with a creditor over the phone because you may feel yourself under pressure to make snap decisions. For this reason it is normally better to continue negotiations by letter, and if your creditor contacts you by phone ask him or her to reply to your letter in writing.

Keeping organised, up-to-date and accurate records of your dealings with creditors is one of the keys to managing your debts effectively. Each time you communicate with a creditor by telephone or in person, write a brief summary of the conversation noting down any pertinent details. You will be able to refer back to the notes that you made if you have a dispute with your creditor at a later date. Add information about payments that you have made, the date that you made them and the reducing balance. This will allow you to see exactly what you owe at any point in time.

Debt management companies and free alternatives

Daunted by the prospect of negotiating with their creditors, some people turn to debt management companies (DMCs) which offer to do this on your behalf, in return for a hefty set-up fee and a share of your monthly repayments (typically 15 per cent, plus VAT). As well as removing the hassle of dealing with creditors, these firms also promise to reduce your monthly payments to a sum you can afford. Unfortunately, the performance of many DMCs leaves a lot to be desired. The way they tackle debts often does little to solve their customers' financial difficulties and, in some cases, the fees they charge may even make things worse.

The main problem with debt management companies is that they sometimes ignore priority debts, such as mortgages, rent arrears and utility bills. Customers are left to deal with these themselves, while DMCs tackle non-priority creditors. Their strategy is to reduce monthly outgoings by spreading payments over a longer period and persuading creditors to freeze interest and charges. This may bring temporary relief, where creditors agree, but you are still left liable for the full amount of your original debt. You are also liable for the DMC's own charges, which are often substantial.

A common criticism of debt management companies is that they fail to make a proper assessment of their clients' financial positions. Some also fail to forward payments promptly, damaging their clients' credit ratings and leaving them exposed to high interest rates and charges.

Rather than paying for the services of a debt management company, most people would do better to turn to other sources of help. The Citizens Advice Bureaux (CAB)*, the

Consumer Credit Counselling Service (CCCS)* and National Debtline* are free services that provide debt advice. Like debt management companies, the CCCS and CAB can negotiate with your creditors to reduce your monthly payments. The National Debtline provides a self-help pack that can help you put together a financial statement and a list of creditors. It may then refer you to either the CCCS or PayPlan*, another free debt management service. Other money advisors can be located through the Federation of Information Advice Centres*.

CHAPTER 3

Priority debts

A priority debt is one that will cause you a considerable degree of hardship if it remains unpaid. Failure to satisfy priority creditors may lead to homelessness, imprisonment or being deprived of essential goods and services. The degree of priority that you should give to any debt will depend not on its size but on the severity of the penalty involved if you do not repay it.

The main priority debts are:

- mortgages and other secured loans
- rent arrears
- gas and electricity bills
- council tax and community charge arrears
- fines and court orders
- maintenance and child support orders
- income tax and VAT
- National Insurance contributions
- hire purchase creditors (in certain cases).

Mortgage arrears

Failing to pay your monthly mortgage payments puts your home at risk – and your lender may be able to evict you and sell your home. This is known as repossession. However, repossession doesn't happen automatically. The lender will contact you first by phone and then write to you before referring the case to lawyers and finally issuing a summons in the County Court. It is possible to negotiate at every stage – contact the Citizens Advice Bureau (CAB)★ for help and advice.

If you are having problems paying your mortgage, you should contact your lender straight away and explain your difficulties. The longer the problem is left, the harder it will be to deal with. Mortgage lenders employ a range of staff who deal with problems relating to arrears and will normally prefer to come to an arrangement with the borrower rather than taking possession proceedings.

The Banking and Mortgage Codes, agreed by the British Bankers Association (BBA)★, the Building Societies Association★, the Association for Payment Clearing Services★ and the Council of Mortgage Lenders★, commit lenders to dealing sympathetically with people in arrears. They also commit lenders to allowing a debt counsellor (from an organisation such as the CAB)★ to negotiate with them on your behalf if you have authorised this. The BBA produces a booklet, *Dealing with debt: how your bank can help*, which you might find useful.

Six strategies for dealing with mortgage arrears

1. Only pay back the interest on the loan

If you have a repayment mortgage and you are unable to keep up with your regular mortgage repayments, you could ask the lender if it is prepared to let you make payments on an 'interest only' basis. This means that you make reduced repayments which cover the interest charged on the loan but not the capital sum borrowed. If you have an endowment, pension or ISA mortgage, you can freeze payments to the 'investment' so that you are only paying interest on the mortgage.

Advantages:
- you will have less to pay back each month
- you can go back to making your usual payments when your income increases.

Disadvantages:
- the loan may take longer to repay
- the arrangement will not take into account any arrears that have already accrued. If you have built up arrears, your lender may suggest that your payments be increased to cover the repayment of these, unless your financial statement shows that this is impracticable.
- during the time that you are only paying interest your loan is not reducing. This may cause you problems in the future.

If you decide to opt for this strategy you should make the lender aware that it is only a temporary solution to your problem, and that you will go back to making your normal repayments as soon as your situation has improved. The lender may set a review date to re-examine your circumstances.

2. Negotiate a payment reduction with your lender

Mortgage lenders are sometimes amenable to an arrangement that will enable you to pay back less than your normal mortgage repayments. This may be cheaper to a creditor than the costs involved in repossessing the property. Repayments are also more likely to be maintained if they are set at a lower level. The following are ways in which you might be able to get the lender to agree to reduce your monthly repayments:

- ask the lender if it is prepared to extend the period of the loan, while reducing repayments to make them more affordable. You should bear in mind that if the loan is

extended in this way, the total amount that you will have to pay back may ultimately be greater.
- ask the lender to charge a lower rate of interest, either for a fixed period or for the rest of the loan.

3. Combine together all your secured debt (loan consolidation)

If you have taken out a secured loan with a second lender (at a high rate of interest) alongside your mortgage (which charges a lower rate), and you are finding it difficult to keep up both sets of repayments, it may be worth speaking to your first lender to arrange a refinancing deal to incorporate both loans into one. The effect of this will be to reduce your monthly repayments. The deal will be much easier to arrange if you have a good track record of making payments to your first lender even if you have missed payments to the second.

Although the arrangement will result in you paying back less money each month, it is important to remember that there will be charges for setting up the new loan and that payments may extend over a longer period than the original agreement. Some secured lenders also make penalty charges if you decide to settle up early.

4. Combine arrears with the remaining loan (capitalise arrears)

If you have built up mortgage arrears during a period of difficulty but are now able to resume regular repayments due to an improvement in your circumstances, you can ask your lender to add the unpaid arrears to the outstanding capital sum and charge you interest on the resulting amount. This will make the burden of arrears less onerous and leave you more funds to pay other priority debts.

Advantages:
- arrears are no longer treated as an unpaid debt
- no further action will be taken against you
- repayments are affordable.

Disadvantages:
- repayments increase if the term of the loan remains unaltered
- the new debt may take longer to pay off
- you will be paying interest on the arrears throughout the remaining term of the loan.

5. Apply for tenant status under the Mortgage Rescue Scheme

This is a little-known strategy of changing from homeowner to tenant status while continuing to live in your own home. The way that it works is that your local housing association will buy your home and will settle the balance outstanding on the mortgage with your lender. This will allow you to continue to reside at your property while making payments to the housing association. You will also have the chance to buy your house back if your finances improve. Unfortunately, rescue schemes are rare, but it is worth checking with your local authority to see if such schemes exist in your area and whether you meet their criteria.

6. Sell your home

Although it is a last resort, you may, in certain circumstances, decide to sell your home to meet priority debt repayments. If you intend to sell up, your lender may extend its deadline for repossession.

Advantages:
- if repossession appears inevitable and you have some equity in your home, you will probably get a better price

for it by selling it on the open market. Inhabited houses tend to sell more quickly and at a better price than repossessed properties

- if your current home is in a particularly expensive area, or is larger than meets your needs, it might be worth selling it and moving into a smaller house or to a cheaper area
- if there is a considerable amount of equity in your property, you may be able to realise a high enough lump sum following its sale to clear your priority debts in full. The money that you can raise from the sale of the property will also be useful to clear pressing business debts or loans from friends and family.

Disadvantages:
- if you need your local council to rehouse you, following the sale, it will be tricky explaining to the council that by selling your home you were not trying to make yourself intentionally homeless
- once you have sold your home to meet debt repayments it will be difficult to get back on the property ladder if you want to buy again
- there may be considerable fees and expenses associated with buying and selling property. For more information see *Which? Way to Buy, Sell and Move House* available from Which? Books*.

In most cases you should only consider selling your home to pay back debts if there is no other alternative. Remember that non-priority debts such as loans, overdrafts and credit-card debts are not secured on your property and can be dealt with without having to sell your home. Chapter 4 provides useful strategies for dealing with unsecured debt.

Possession proceedings (for mortgage or rent arrears)

If you continue to fail to pay your mortgage or rent without reaching any compromise agreement, after giving you due warning your mortgage lender or landlord may issue a County Court claim requesting possession of the property.

Along with a summons giving a time and date for the hearing and other court papers, the court will normally send you a list of advice agencies. If you have not done so already, get help and advice from these straight away.

It is important that you give considerable thought to completing the reply form. You should bear the following in mind.

- If possession is granted to the landlord, you will have just 14 days in which to move out. If this short notice is likely to be insufficient to enable you to find alternative accommodation, you should mention it in your response.
- If you have been unable to keep up payments because you are experiencing financial problems that will soon be rectified (e.g. you have just found a new job or the council has agreed to pay you Housing Benefit), you should make this should be make known to the court.
- Include details of your personal circumstances, in particular if you are sick or have a disability or you have young children living with you.
- If you are entitled to claim Housing Benefit, but you have not been receiving payments from the local authority, you should mention this to the court (see Chapter 9 for more on housing benefit). If possible, you should obtain a letter from the local authority advising that it is prepared to meet the contractual payments, as well as providing payment of arrears.

The court hearing

At the court, you will have to explain your situation and intentions to a judge. It is vital that you attend so that you can put forward your defence. You should also ask an adviser to represent you at the hearing.

The court will need to satisfy itself that you have missed payments, and that your landlord or mortgage lender has used the proper procedures when trying to get the money you owe. If your landlord has not carried out his or her obligations (for example, repairing your house or flat), the court may not make a possession order.

If you are a local authority (council) tenant, the court will take account of whether you are vulnerable (for example, if you are elderly) and whether you have tried to make payments.

In the case of mortgage arrears, in order to suspend a possession order the court will need to be satisfied that you will continue to make basic payments to the lender, while paying instalments to clear the mortgage arrears within 'a reasonable period'.

If you have a spouse or partner who lives with you, he or she will be treated as a co-defendant, and will be able to put forward his or her own defence in court.

If your landlord or mortgage lender proves their case, then the court usually grants a possession order. However, if you start paying the money you owe, you normally won't be evicted. If you subsequently miss payments, the landlord or mortgage lender can ask for an eviction warrant. You can request a court hearing asking the judge to call off (suspend) the eviction by completing Form N245 and sending it to the court (enclose a financial statement on a separate sheet if it helps your case). If a warrant is granted, the court will instruct the bailiffs to evict you. If this happens you should seek help and advice immediately. If you have nowhere to live, contact your landlord and try to extend the date.

Repossession

If you are unable to reach an agreement with your mortgage lender and your home is repossessed, keep a close eye on the prices that similar properties are being sold for in your area. You may be able to appeal if the lender sells the property for less than the market value (see below). You will also need to bear in mind that legal costs, unpaid mortgage payments and other costs will be added to the debt up to the point that the property is sold. If you are unhappy about the way that you have been treated by your lender – for instance it has sold your home for less than the market value, you might consider taking your complaint to the Mortgage Code Arbitration Scheme★ or the Financial Ombudsman Service★. (For further details see the Council of Mortgage Lenders★ website.)

Mortgage shortfall debt

If the lender has repossessed your home and sold your property for less than the amount of the loan, you may find yourself facing a demand for the repayment of the shortfall. This may not come for several years after the sale. Until recently, mortgage lenders could chase borrowers for payment of the shortfall debt for up to 12 years. Although this period has now been reduced to six years it can be extended if the lender makes you aware of the shortfall before this period elapses. If you receive a demand for a mortgage shortfall after a period of six years, you should seek advice from a debt specialist or solicitor to clarify the actual period that has elapsed to see if you have a good case for challenging the debt.

There are several ways of challenging this shortfall debt although you will need to contact a specialist solicitor to act on your behalf. The following arguments may be used in the negotiation process:

- The lender was negligent in looking after the property after repossession, for example neglecting simple maintenance and keeping the garden tidy, which could have influenced the saleability of the property.
- The lender sold the property for an amount considerably below its market value at the time. The property must have either been sold through an estate agent in the normal way, or at auction for a price that reflected the market value of the property at the time.
- The sale was unnecessarily delayed, which caused the mortgage interest to rise and the shortfall to increase.

A mortgage shortfall debt is a non-priority debt, and the lender's powers to collect are no greater than those for credit-card debts or bank overdrafts. Many mortgage lenders are unlikely to enforce the shortfall debt rigorously and it will usually be easier to come to an alternative arrangement. You might consider employing one of the following strategies:

- **Ask for a write-off** This is the best strategy if you are on a low income or in receipt of benefit, and your circumstances are unlikely to improve in the near future. Pages 69–70 give details of how to go about asking for a write-off.
- **Offer the lender a payment in full and final settlement** Lenders routinely accept repayments of less

than the full amount of the shortfall debt in full and final settlement, and reductions of more than 50 per cent of the debt are not uncommon. You should ask a debt adviser or solicitor to negotiate on your behalf to ensure that you receive the maximum reduction available.

- **Offer token instalment payments** Many lenders are happy to accept small instalment payments towards the shortfall debt because this shows a willingness to repay the sum owed. It can, however, be demoralising to pay a negligible amount (say £15 per month towards a debt of £20,000), because the debt seems to be hanging over your head for life. One strategy is to keep up payments to your lender for a while and then follow this up with a request for a write-off or lump sum in full and final settlement.

The mortgage indemnity guarantee

The mortgage indemnity guarantee (MIG) is a lump sum payment you make at the time the mortgage is taken out if the amount you borrowed is greater than 90 to 95 per cent of the lender's valuation of the property. The MIG insures the lender against loss if there is a shortfall after the property is subsequently repossessed.

If your home is repossessed, you will need to check with the mortgage company that it has made a claim under the insurance policy because this may limit your losses. Note that you may be liable for any payment made by the insurer to the mortgage company – a process known as subrogation. It is recommended that you speak to a solicitor if you are being chased for subrogation by an insurer.

Rent arrears

If you live in rented accommodation it is important that you keep up payments on your rent because if you do not you can be evicted for rent arrears and face the possibility of having nowhere to live.

Most landlords do not want to evict tenants unless they have a good reason for doing so. The first step should be to get in touch with your landlord to make him or her aware of the problems that you are facing in order that these might be resolved without the landlord resorting to court action. You may find that you can come to an understanding without too much aggravation.

If you are in receipt of Housing Benefit, you can arrange to have this paid directly to your landlord. This might make your landlord more willing to come to an arrangement over your arrears because he or she will be sure of receiving regular payments. Similarly, a sum from Income Support or Jobseeker's Allowance can be paid directly to your landlord towards rent arrears.

If your landlord (whether a private landlord, the council or a housing association) wants you to leave because you have failed to pay your rent, you have the right to stay in your home in most cases until the landlord gets a court order called a 'possession order'.

Normally landlords must give you notice that they want to end the tenancy. If you do not leave by the end of the notice period, the landlord can start 'possession proceedings' in the County Court. You do not have to leave at the end of the notice period, but you may have to pay the landlord's costs of going to court if you don't.

If the court awards an 'outright possession' order, and you still do not leave, the landlord can ask the court to call in bailiffs to evict you.

In some cases, a court may grant a 'suspended order', which allows the tenant to stay in his or her home as long as he or she pays off a certain amount each month or week. Alternatively it may order an 'adjournment', where the hearing is put off, as long as the tenant agrees to pay a certain amount.

Your specific rights depend largely on the type of tenancy agreement you have. However, if you share the living space with your landlord (which could mean a kitchen or bathroom, but not just a hall, staircase or entrance), the landlord can evict you without going to court. The landlord must usually give you four weeks' notice, either spoken or in writing.

Types of tenancy agreements

There are three types of tenancy agreements:

- a regulated (or 'protected') tenancy
- an assured tenancy
- an assured shorthold tenancy.

The type of tenancy you have depends mainly on when it was taken out. Most private tenancies which started before 15 January 1989 are regulated (or protected) tenancies. This type of tenancy has the most protection against rent increases or eviction.

If the tenancy started between 15 January 1989 and 27 February 1997, it will be an 'assured shorthold tenancy' if the landlord made this clear on a special legal form at the beginning. Otherwise it will be an 'assured tenancy'. The tenancy must have had an initial fixed term of at least six months.

Tenancy agreements started on or after 28 February 1997 are 'assured shorthold tenancies', unless the landlord has said in writing that it is an 'assured tenancy'. The tenancy may start either with a fixed period or as a 'periodic' tenancy which runs from week to week or from month to month (depending on when rent is paid). Either way, the tenant has the right to stay for at least six months.

If you are unsure what type of tenancy you have, check your tenancy agreement. If you don't have one, ask your landlord for a copy of it.

Regulated tenancies

The landlord must first end the tenancy by giving the tenant a 'notice to quit' (unless an end date was agreed at the start of the tenancy). This must give you at least four weeks' notice and be in a special legal form. The landlord must then apply to the court for a possession order. There are certain 'mandatory' grounds, for which the court will automatically grant possession, as well as 'discretionary' grounds, for which the court must decide whether it is reasonable to evict the tenant (see 'Assured tenancies', below).

Assured tenancies

With an assured tenancy, the landlord must first give the tenant a legal notice, called a 'notice of seeking possession'. If you are a tenant, and you get a notice like this, you should get advice immediately.

Depending on the reasons ('grounds') for possession, the landlord must give you either two weeks' or two months' notice that he or she intends to apply for a possession order. (If the landlord also claims you have behaved 'anti-socially', he or she can start possession proceedings immediately after giving notice.)

You may either go to court and argue against the landlord's claim (that is, that he doesn't have the right to end the tenancy); or wait to see if the court issues a possession order.

Landlords must first prove to the court that they have a reason for possession. In certain cases (known as 'mandatory grounds') the court will automatically grant possession. These include where you are at least two months or eight weeks behind with the rent. Other grounds are 'discretionary'. This means the court will decide whether or not it is reasonable to grant possession. The most common discretionary grounds include where you have missed rent payments.

Assured shorthold tenancies

People with assured shorthold tenancies have less protection than assured tenants. After six months, the landlord can get a possession order from the court (without having to show any grounds for doing so).

Within the first six months of the tenancy, the landlord can get possession only if he or she can show a ground for eviction, in the same way as for an assured tenancy. Your landlord must give you at least two months' notice that he or she wants possession, and cannot go to court until that notice period has been completed. But as long as the landlord has followed the procedures properly, the court will automatically grant possession.

The landlord can apply to use the 'accelerated possession' procedure, which allows him or her to apply for possession without having to attend a hearing. But he or she can't use this in the case of unpaid rent. And in any case, the tenant can still ask for a possession order to be delayed if it would cause 'exceptional' hardship.

Harassment by a landlord

It is generally illegal for a landlord to evict a tenant without a court order – which includes changing locks while the tenant is out, for example. However, there are a few situations where the tenant does not have this protection. The most common is where the tenant shares the living space with his or her landlord.

If you are a tenant who is being harassed, or you are facing illegal eviction by a private landlord, contact the tenancy relations officer at your local council (or whoever else there deals with harassment and illegal eviction). The council officer should try to stop the harassment and persuade the landlord to let you back into your home. If this fails, the council can prosecute the landlord.

Tenants can also take action in the court themselves, though expert legal help is needed to do this. A tenant can apply for an injunction to stop the landlord harassing him or her or to let the tenant return to his or her home. The tenant should also be able to claim compensation. If the case is urgent, the tenant can get an emergency injunction before there is a fuller court hearing.

The Protection from Harassment Act 1997 also offers protection against harassment by a landlord, even where the landlord is not necessarily directly trying to evict a tenant.

Gas and electricity bills

If you cannot pay your gas or electricity bills, the companies involved will usually try to come to an agreement on clearing the debt and will disconnect you only if this fails. Depending on the extent of your other debts, you may be allowed to pay off your outstanding bill in instalments before the next bill is due. However, if there is not enough money for you to do this, ask whether there is a monthly budget scheme which would enable you to spread what you owe over a period of time (depending on the size of the arrears). Alternatively, you could have prepayment meters installed. The meter is set to charge enough to clear what is outstanding as well as the normal cost of use and standing charges.

What can I do if threatened with disconnection?

If your gas or electricity supplier is threatening disconnection, you might consider the following options.

- Contact the supplier and ask for more time to pay. You are likely to be able to come to an arrangement unless you have not honoured previous extensions.
- If you are a pensioner, or have a pensioner living with you in your home, you cannot be disconnected during the winter months. If you are in this position you should inform social services who will negotiate with the utility company on your behalf. You will also be given extra consideration if you have a child under 11 or a person with a disability living with you.
- It may be worth contacting Energywatch* or the regulatory body, OFGEM* which might be able to intervene.

Council tax and community charge

If you haven't paid your council tax, the council will apply for a 'liability order' in the magistrates court. This means the council can use bailiffs to get the money from you (by taking things of value that you own), or take money from your wages or benefits. For this reason, if you owe money it is important that you contact your local council immediately so that you can reach an agreement on how you can pay back the arrears.

If you are unable to pay the entire amount in one payment, you should offer to pay by instalments. The council will measure your ability to pay by sending you a means-test form, which asks you to detail the income and outgoings of you and your partner, and whether either of you owns a car. The information that you give on the form will enable the council to decide on how much you can afford to pay back each month. If your income fluctuates, because you are self-employed or a salesperson earning commission, avoid over-stating the amount that you earn.

If you are having difficulty paying your council tax because you are on a low income or you are out of work, you might find that you are entitled to claim council tax benefit. Contact your local Benefits Agency or JobCentre for advice (see Chapter 9 for more on benefits).

It is also worth checking whether you could ask for lower council tax payments, or whether you should have to pay council tax at all (council tax exemption). There are different ways you might be able to reduce what you owe. Examples include:

- claiming backdated Council Tax Benefit over the past 52 weeks if you have been on a low income
- asking to have your house or flat revalued (if it is revalued into a lower council tax band, you will pay less council tax).

There are other circumstances where you may not have to pay or could make lower payments. Contact your local CAB★ for further help.

Fines and court orders

These debts cannot be ignored because failure to pay can lead to the bailiffs taking action against you or even imprisonment if the court feels that there has been a wilful refusal to pay back the debt. If your financial position means you cannot pay a fine, you can ask to be allowed to pay it by instalments.

What happens if I have a court fine that I cannot afford to pay?

It is possible to pay a fine by instalments, over time. You will need to apply to the court where the fine was issued in order to put forward your case.

When you make your application to the court you will be required to complete a form that asks you to detail your income and expenditure. The court will then decide on the amount and duration of the instalments, or whether the fine should be written off completely.

The court will fix a date on which to check that you have made payments according to the new schedule. If you default, the court may involve the bailiffs. You should contact the court immediately if there are extenuating circumstances that should be taken into accout.

Maintenance and child support orders

The Child Support Agency (CSA)* can collect arrears in payments by authorising your employer to make deductions from your wages, or it can apply to the magistrates' court for a liability order. This can lead to sanctions such as seizing money direct from your bank account (a garnishee order) or putting a charge on your house (a charging order). If you cannot meet child support payments you should contact the CSA and ask to be reassessed.

Income tax and VAT

Income tax

The Inland Revenue★ has wide-ranging powers to collect unpaid tax, especially if it believes that the reason for the non-payment was wilful refusal to pay.

If you are late submitting your tax return or paying tax due you can be fined and ordered to pay a sum that has been calculated by the Tax Office.

Enforcement measures that can be used by the Inland Revenue include:

- County Court action, which may include an attachment of earnings, third-party debt order, instalment order, charging order etc., based on your circumstances. (For more information, see Chapter 7)
- a magistrates' court order
- commencing bankruptcy proceedings against you (see Chapter 6)
- issuing a warrant for the seizure of your goods by bailiffs. The Inland Revenue does not need to apply to the County Court to recover goods through bailiffs (see Chapter 8).

VAT

HM Customs and Excise★ acts promptly to collect outstanding VAT. If you are late sending in your VAT return you may have to pay a fee.

The first step taken by Customs and Excise to collect unpaid VAT is to send a letter demanding immediate payment. This is backed up with the threat of bailiff action to recover the unpaid amount. Customs and Excise has the power to make you bankrupt if it is unable to recover the amount owed through bailiff action.

If you are unable to pay back the VAT, you should contact Customs and Excise to negotiate payment by instalments. Make them aware of the hardship that you are currently facing and back this up with a statement showing your financial situation. If a bailiff has already gained access to your business premises or home, it may be better to pay up in full to prevent your goods from being seized.

National Insurance contributions

Class 2 and Class 4 National Insurance contributions (for the self-employed) are a priority debt as they are assessed and collected by the Inland Revenue, together with unpaid income tax.

Hire purchase creditors

If you buy goods under hire purchase (HP) – usually cars or furniture – or a similar scheme, known as a 'conditional sale agreement', you don't own the goods until you have made the final payment. Until then, they belong to the creditor (the finance company).

A hire purchase debt is a priority debt only if it is essential that you retain the item in question – for example, a car for work – because goods secured under the agreement are at risk if you fail to repay the loan.

If you miss payments before you've paid a third of the total amount you owe (this figure will be on the front of your agreement), the creditor can 'snatch back' the item. They can do this only if it is in a public place, so they may be able to repossess a car, but they cannot come into your home and take furniture.

If you have paid a third or more of the total amount you owe, the creditor must start court action to get the goods back, or to get you to pay. You will then receive a hearing date, when the court will decide whether you must return the item or accept any offer to make payment that you have made.

You can ask for a 'time order', under which the court can reduce the payments to a level you can afford (see page 00). The court can make a 'suspended order', which means that the finance company can get the goods back only if you miss payments.

If you want to avoid court action, you can write to the creditor to end your contract. You will have to pay only half of the total amount you owe (this figure will be on the front of your HP agreement), and the cost of repairing any damage to the goods. But you will have to return the goods.

CHAPTER 4

Non-priority debts

Non-priority debts are those where failure to pay will not result in the loss of your liberty, home or essential goods and services. This is because non-priority creditors cannot apply the same sanctions as priority creditors.

The following are non-priority debts:
- bank overdrafts and loans
- credit-card arrears
- store-card arrears
- catalogue arrears (including mail order)
- hire purchase arrears (non-essential goods)
- benefit overpayments.

As we have seen in Chapter 2, non-priority debts should only be paid after priority creditors have been satisfied. This does not mean that they should be ignored, or that non-priority creditors have no legal redress, simply that the most pressing debts have first call on available funds.

If, after dealing with priority debts as suggested in Chapter 3, you cannot afford to make the repayments your remaining creditors demand, there are several strategies you can use to negotiate with them.

Eight strategies for dealing with non-priority debts

1. Suspend repayments to your creditors

If you are short of money because you are out of work or you need to use your income to pay off some pressing arrears to your priority creditors, a useful tactic is to ask non-priority creditors to delay action to recover the debt and freeze the interest for a few months to give you enough time to sort out your problems.

This strategy is particularly suitable when your income has stopped temporarily but will be resuming soon or if you need time to sell some assets to raise funds.

Advantages:

- it can provide a much-needed breathing space to enable you to get your finances back in order
- asking for a hold-off can give you time to work out the best strategy for dealing with your debts
- if you are out of work it can give you time to find the right job rather than being forced to take the first one that you find
- it keeps creditors informed about your situation.

Disadvantages:

- it is not a permanent solution. After the delay you will be expected to resume payments as before
- some creditors will keep charging interest on the debt.

You need to make it clear to your creditors why you have found yourself in this situation and be able to justify the payments delay that you are asking for. When you write to your creditors you should enclose a financial statement (see pages 21–3) and ask for written confirmation that collection action and interest charges will cease.

Sample letter requesting a delay in payments

XYZ Collections

Surrey

Dear Sir or Madam,

Last week my employer, Smith Electronics, was declared insolvent and I was unfortunately laid off without redundancy pay. I anticipate that it will take me at least three months to find another job, so during this period I will only be receiving Income Support. As my financial statement shows, I owe my creditors a total of £20,000, so I am writing to you and the rest of my creditors to ask you to hold off any collection action and interest charges for at least the next four months until the end of July. I will of course let you know immediately should my circumstances change for the better or worse.

   I hope that you will appreciate that my request is not unreasonable in the circumstances and is the only realistic way that I can continue to survive during this difficult period. Please let me know of your decision in writing as soon as possible.

Yours truly,

Name

2. Propose a creditor repayment plan

Non-priority creditors will often be prepared to allow you to reduce your monthly payments and settle your debts over a longer period than originally specified. To determine how much you should offer each creditor, you need to draw up a 'creditor repayment plan' showing how much you can afford for payments of this kind and how you propose to divide the total between various creditors.

This strategy, based on the equitable distribution of available income, is suitable when you have a regular income but so much non-priority debt that you are finding it almost impossible to make the necessary monthly repayments. By adopting it you remain committed to paying your creditors back in full.

Advantages:

- by restructuring your payments, you will be able to bring your finances back under your control
- this arrangement is usually endorsed by the County Court because it works on the same principles as an administration order (see pages 61–2)
- by initiating negotiations with creditors yourself, you will not be incurring the high fees charged by a debt management company or insolvency practitioner.

Disadvantages:

- reducing your monthly payment will mean that your debts will take a lot longer to repay
- some creditors will be reluctant to agree to the arrangement.

How to prepare a creditor repayment plan

By following the steps outlined in Chapter 2, you will have already created a clear financial statement (see the example on pages 21–3). If you have any money left over at the end of the month after meeting your living expenses and priority debts, this can form the basis of a creditor repayment plan. The example below shows a monthly surplus of £170 from which to repay non-priority creditors.

In order to persuade your creditors to agree to accept the repayment plan, you must demonstrate that you are treating them equitably. The way to do this is to divide the income you have available to pay non-priority debts between all your non-priority creditors so that each receives a fair share of what is available, based on the size of each debt (a pro-rata basis).

Example of a creditor repayment plan		
Unsecured creditor	Amount owed to creditors (£)	Revised monthly payment (£)*
ABC Finance	8,000	40.60
XYZ Finance	6,500	32.99
Visa card	4,000	20.30
MasterCard	3,000	15.22
Flexible Friend	2,500	12.69
Flexible Foe	5,000	25.37
Ring Your Neck Telecoms	200	1.01
Great White Collection Co.	2,000	10.15
Raining Stones Solicitors	800	4.06
Getcha Inc. Debt Recovery	1,200	6.09
Speeding fines	300	1.52
Total unsecured debts	**33,500**	**170.00**

*Figures for the revised monthly payments are obtained by dividing the money owed to each creditor by the total debt (£33,500) and multiplying this by the disposable income (£170).

The next step is to try to get your creditors to agree to your proposal. In the letter that accompanies your financial statement and creditor repayment plan you should:

- explain why you cannot afford to make full repayment
- present a clear picture of your total debts and available income (financial statement)
- emphasise that you are committed to treating each creditor equitably
- ask the creditor to accept a reduced repayment or, if your offer is zero and you cannot afford any repayment, to accept no payments
- make a request to have the interest on the debt frozen so that your debt does not increase
- point out that other creditors have accepted your offers (if this is true) – this can be a useful point in your favour
- undertake to contact the creditor again when your circumstances improve and you are able to increase your repayments.

Sample letter to creditor offering reduced payments by instalments

ABC Finance

10 High Street

London

Dear Sir or Madam

I am writing to you to explain the problems that I have been facing of late and to suggest an alternative strategy to which I hope you will be able to give your full consideration.

Since taking out the loan in March last year, my fortunes have changed markedly, and owing to factors outside my control I am no longer able to keep up with the payments under the agreement. I hope you will appreciate that at present I have to manage my money carefully in order to eat and keep a roof over my head.

As my financial statement indicates, after deducting money spent on essentials and payments to priority creditors, I have just £170.00 left with which to pay back my other creditors. Because I intend treating all of my creditors fairly, I propose making a revised payment to you of £40.60, which represents 23.88% of my available income. In addition, I also ask you to stop charging interest on my account to prevent my situation from deteriorating still further.

Please contact me in writing to let me know of your decision. I am of course committed to paying all of my creditors back in full and consider that my proposal offers a fair and equitable means of doing so. I also intend to keep you abreast of my situation and will increase my repayment as soon as I have the means of doing so.

Yours faithfully,

Name

What happens if a creditor refuses to co-operate?

You need to remember that your creditors are under no
obligation to alter the original agreement and, although
some will probably accept your proposal straight away,
there are almost certainly going to be others who will not.
These creditors will threaten to keep charging interest,
make late payment charges and even to take you to court
unless regular payments are kept up. You should deal with
this situation by:

- asking them to reconsider
- telling them that other creditors have accepted your offers
- getting help from a free debt advice agency.

How to persuade creditors to accept your plan

- Be polite and courteous at all times.
- Don't crumble under pressure and don't agree to every
  demand that the creditor makes.
- Send the creditor your revised payment, even if it hasn't
  agreed to accept it. This will show that you are committed
  to your proposal. In many cases the creditor will cash the
  cheque and start to go along with the new payment plan.

Recording repayments

If your creditors agree to reduced payments, it can seem a
little depressing when you consider the amount of time
that it will take before the debt is paid off. After six months
to a year have gone by, however, you'll see the remaining
total steadily shrinking and your debts will finally be back
under control.

Specimen repayment record

ABC Finance	Date	Payments	Balance
23/3/03: Jill phoned from			8,000.00
accounts. We discussed my	25/3/03	40.60	7,959.40
situation but she was unable	30/4/03	40.60	7,918.80
to make a decision.	31/5/03	40.60	7,878.20
Promised to call back	30/6/03	40.60	7,837.60
24/3/03: Jill phoned again.			
Tried to insist that I paid			
more but I stood firm on			
my original offer			
25/3/03: Spoke to manager			
who reluctantly agreed to			
accept my revised payment.			
Forwarded payment today.			
Next payment due by 30/4			

3. Set up an administration order

An administration order is a County Court order that calls for the division of your disposable income equitably amongst your creditors in a similar way to a pro-rata creditor repayment plan. Once the order has been set up, it will have the affect of preventing individual creditors from pursuing you further. You will make agreed repayments to the court rather than direct to creditors (see Chapter 7 for further details).

When to use this strategy

An administration order can be made if your total debts do not exceed £5,000 and you have at least one County Court Judgment (CCJ) (see page 122) in your name. It is an appropriate strategy if you don't have much money left over after paying your essential bills and your debts are troublesome but not high enough to warrant bankruptcy.

Advantages:

- once the administration order has been set up, creditors will not be able to chase you for payment directly
- you can also include some priority debts, such as court fines and council tax arrears, in the arrangement (see pages 47–9).

Disadvantages:

- you can set up an administration order only if you owe less than £5,000 to unsecured creditors
- you will have to pay an administration fee on each payment that you make.

4. Offer a lump-sum payment in full and final settlement of the debt

Your creditors can sometimes be persuaded to accept one-off payments of less than the total debt you owe them, if it is made clear that this is the best return they can expect to receive. They are more likely to agree to a lump-sum payment than to write off the debt altogether.

The basis of a settlement is that the lump sum available is divided between your non-priority creditors in proportion to the size of the debt you owe each one.

When to use this strategy

This strategy is suitable when your assets, or the equity in your home, are insufficient to repay all your debts, but you have a lump sum at your disposal, or assets you can sell, which might satisfy your creditors. If your income has reduced to the point where you have no money left over after paying your essential expenses, and you can demonstrate that your financial situation is likely to remain static or worsen over the coming months, your creditors may accept that bankruptcy is your only other option. It is vital that you get the creditor's acceptance in writing, and contact a solicitor to ensure that the acceptance letter is legally binding on your creditor.

Advantages:
- a lump-sum payment agreement provides an opportunity to clear all your unsecured debt in one go
- the strategy is a more attractive option to your creditors than bankruptcy, because in bankruptcy much of the lump sum would be swallowed up in fees.

Disadvantages:
- your creditor may resume action to recover all of the debt after becoming aware of your assets
- the creditor may agree with your proposal and accept your cash sum, but later renege on the agreement and demand that you pay the rest of the debt. You will be able to deal with this if you have already obtained agreement in writing (see above)
- you will not have a lump sum to spend on essentials such as food, repairs and housing.

Sample letter offering a lump-sum payment in full and final settlement

Flexible Foe Visa Company

A/C no 1234 5678

Dear Sir or Madam,

In April last year I was forced out of business because of a fall-off in demand. I live in a small flat with a large mortgage and possess few assets of any value. I have recently signed on and I am currently receiving Jobseeker's allowance.

As my financial statement demonstrates, I owe my creditors a total of £35,000. My last account from you showed that I still owe you £5,000, which represents 1/7th of the total. I am currently in the process of cashing a number of shares that I still hold from my last job which will release a total of £7,000, and by dividing this amount equitably among my creditors, I can make you an immediate payment of £1,000. In return, I ask that you accept this payment in full and final settlement of the money that I owe you and that you send me a letter to this effect so that I will be able to keep my side of the bargain.

I hope that you will agree that my offer is reasonable in the circumstances. Please let me know in writing when you have made your decision.

Yours faithfully,

Name

5. Offer a lump sum with instalments

This is a similar strategy to offering a lump sum in full and final payment but more attractive to creditors as they receive continuing, albeit reduced, repayments towards the rest of the debt.

When to use this strategy

You should adopt this course of action when you have some capital or realisable assets and a regular income but your normal repayments are too high to meet in full. In exchange for a lump sum and the promise of continuing, though reduced, payments your creditor may agree to forgo further action against you and perhaps to freeze interest charges. As with other strategies, it is important to get the creditor's agreement in writing.

Advantages:
- repayments are reduced
- creditor takes no further sanctions.

Disadvantages:
- your assets are reduced, allowing you less flexibility
- continued demand for regular repayments.

6. Ask your creditors to partially write off the debt

Creditors may agree to reduce the balance owed to a manageable sum, or to accept reduced repayments for two or three years – after which the unpaid sum is written off. This is a similar strategy to a legally enforced Individual Voluntary Arrangement (IVA), see pages 90–3, but means that extra money will be available to pay back creditors instead of being swallowed up in fees.

When to use this strategy

This strategy is suitable if you have some surplus income available to pay creditors, but not enough to clear the whole debt within a reasonable period of time. It is appropriate if you have no valuable assets or no significant equity in your home and do not expect your circumstances to improve.

Advantages:
- repayments are reduced to an achievable amount
- the total debt is reduced
- payments are compressed into a manageable time-frame.

Disadvantages:
- not all creditors may agree to reduced payments
- details of written-off debts may be passed to credit reference agencies, making it harder for you to obtain credit.

Sample letter offering partial write-off

XYZ Collections

Leeds

Dear Sir or Madam,

In April this year, my wife has had to stop working due to illness. We have two young children, and managing our household budget while meeting debt repayments on just my salary is proving to be very difficult if not impossible. I am therefore in no position to keep up my monthly payment of £100 per month and would instead like to propose an alternative strategy for clearing the debt that I hope you will be able to give consideration to.

As the attached financial statement shows, I currently owe my unsecured creditors a total of £10,000. After deducting essential spending, I have calculated that I have just £50 each month left over to pay back my unsecured creditors. My last statement showed that I owe you a total of £2,000, which means after paying my creditors an equal share of the money I have available, £10 per month is the most that I can afford to pay you back at this time.

I'm sure that you'll agree that given the size of my debts and the money that I have available, it is important for me to pay the debt back within a reasonable time period. I therefore propose to continue making payments to you for five years, after which time I ask you to write off the debt completely. I also ask you to stop charging interest on the debt to prevent my finances from deteriorating still further.

I hope that you agree that this solution offers the best chance for you to get back a significant portion of the money that you have lent me. Please let me know in writing when you have made your decision.

Yours faithfully,

Name

7. Ask your creditors to write off the complete debt

This strategy is likely to succeed only if you can demonstrate to your creditors that you have no means of paying them back and that any enforcement action they take will end in failure.

When to use this strategy

Asking for your debts to be written off is worthwhile if you have little or no income, it is unlikely that your financial situation will improve much in the future and you have very few assets that you can sell to pay back your creditors. For example, you don't own your own home or you have little or no equity in it, and have so much debt that it is unlikely that you will be able to repay it. Bankruptcy is your only other viable alternative.

Advantages:

- if your creditors agree to write off the debt, this strategy presents you with a way of starting a clean slate
- once the debt has been formally written off, you will not owe your creditors anything.

Disadvantages:

- your creditors will need to be completely satisfied that you have no ability to repay your debts, either now or in the future, before they agree to write off the debt
- writing off debts will damage your rating with credit reference agencies.

How to approach your creditors

The best way to approach your creditors is to do so in writing. That way you will be able to set your position out clearly and concisely and stand a greater chance of success. Do not enter into any type of negotiation or commitment until your creditor has been given the opportunity to read your letter and to respond in an appropriate way.

Old debts

Creditors are more likely to agree to write off debts they have been pursuing for a long period without success. If your debt is still fairly new, you should ask the creditor to withold action (and stop interest charges) for three to six months, then follow up with a request for a write-off after this period has elapsed.

Example of a letter requesting a write-off

Debt and Dishonour Finance

100 High Street

London

Dear Sir or Madam,

Thank you for your letter dated 20th December advising me of the £823 balance outstanding on my account. My reason for writing to you is to apologise for letting the debt get out of hand and to offer you an explanation as to why the debt remains unpaid.

Since taking the loan out in July 2000, my situation has altered dramatically. I lost my job last year because of ill health and since then have been unable to work. Apart from sickness benefit of £83.21 per week I have no other income, and as the enclosed financial statement will demonstrate, after paying for food and other essentials I have no money left over with which to pay my creditors. I rent my home and have no other assets of any real value.

My statement shows that I already owe my other unsecured creditors a total of £23,500. My doctor has advised me that I am unlikely to be able to work again for some time and because of this I can see no realistic way in which I can pay you back.

In view of this fact, I am asking you to write off the debt in full. Any further action that you take to recover the debt will not succeed, and in writing off my debt you will help to eliminate the cost of further enforcement action. My local Citizens Advice Bureau has already told me that bankruptcy is my only other viable course of action, and if I fail to get the agreement of my creditors to write off my debts I will have no alternative but to take this option.

I am sorry that things have had to come to this but I really have no other alternative. I would be grateful if you would let me know of your decision, in writing, at your earliest convenience.

Yours sincerely,

Name

If the creditor formally agrees to write off the debt and sends you a written undertaking to confirm the action that it has taken, you can be confident that you have seen an end to the debt and you will not be approached again even if your financial position improves. However, some creditors may never formally agree to writing off your debt but may strike it off their books at some date in the future convenient to them, or will keep it on file in case you have the means to begin repayments in the future.

8. Ask your creditor to accept token instalments

This strategy is appropriate if you have no, or very little, money left to make repayments to your non-priority creditors after paying your essential outgoings and priority debts. If your creditor is not prepared to write off the debt, you can offer to make very small payments (50p a month is sufficient) towards the debt. This saves the creditor from attempting to enforce the debt in the County Court, which would involve additional costs and might have the same outcome.

When to use this strategy

Token instalments may be accepted if you have a very low income and find it difficult to meet basic expenses. You must be able to demonstrate the constraints of your situation from your financial statement.

Advantages:

- you can continue to make payments to your creditors without placing a strain on your budget
- a creditor is much more likely to agree to accept token payments than to agree to a write-off.

Disadvantage:

- once you have acknowledged your intent to pay the debt, the creditor will be less likely to agree to write it off, and so the debt continues to hang over your head.

How to approach your creditors

The first step is to write a letter apologising for allowing the debt to get out of hand and explaining that in your circumstances a small token payment of 50p or £1 per month is all that you can afford to pay. You should demonstrate this by costing out your expenses carefully on a financial statement (see pages 21–3). You should also convey the fact that you are committed to treating all of your creditors fairly and that you will increase your payments as soon as you have the means to do so. Creditors should be made aware that bankruptcy remains your only other viable alternative.

If the creditor agrees to accept your token payments, it is essential that you get confirmation of this in writing. Ask for a payment book, which will allow you to record regular payments.

Sample letter offering payment by token instalments

Raining Stones Collection Company

10 Anshark Ave

Brokelhurst

BPO ORR

A/C no: 69696969/69

Dear Sir or Madam

Thank you for your letter of 25th December 2001 advising me of the £600 arrears on my account and requesting immediate payment. The reason for my writing to you is to explain the problems that I have been facing of late and to suggest an alternative strategy to which I hope you will be able to give your full consideration.

Since taking out the loan in March last year, my fortunes have changed markedly, and I am now no longer in a position

---

to keep up with the payments under the agreement. In August last year I lost my job, and have so far been unsuccessful in finding alternative employment. My difficulties have extended to not being able to pay the rent on my flat and I am dangerously close to being evicted. I also owe other unsecured creditors a total of £15,000, of which I am unable to pay more than a token amount.

As the enclosed financial statement will demonstrate, the maximum amount that I can afford to pay you at this stage is £1 per month, which I will begin paying the moment that I have your agreement. In addition, I also ask you to stop charging interest on my account to prevent my finances from deteriorating still further.

Please contact me in writing to let me know of your decision. I will of course keep you abreast of my situation and will let you know if my situation changes for the better. I am sorry that things have not worked out as I had predicted but promise to do everything that I can to honour our new commitment when I have your agreement in writing.

Yours sincerely,

Name

CHAPTER 5

Student debt

With the abolition of grants and the introduction of student loans, debt has now become an uncomfortable reality faced by nearly all students. Research commissioned by Barclays Bank found that students left university with debts averaging £10,997 in 2002, a figure that is forecast to rise by 13 per cent in 2003 to £12,500.

Student loans

Student loans are the main source of meeting students' living costs. For most students the amount they can borrow will depend on a means-test of their income and that of their parents (or spouse). The bodies that assess your eligibility are your local education authority (LEA) in England and Wales, the Department of Education for Northern Ireland★ in Northern Ireland and the Student Awards Agency for Scotland★ in Scotland. The loan will be paid in three separate instalments (one for each term) by the Student Loans Company★.

All students who are eligible for help can borrow about 75 per cent of the maximum amount of loan available (see table overleaf); the remaining amount will be means-tested. If the amount your parents (or spouse) are asked to contribute is equal to the means-tested part of the loan, you can borrow only up to the figure given for the non-means-tested part. How much you can borrow also depends on where you study and whether or not you live at home. Loans are lower in the final year of study because they do not cover the summer holidays.

A higher rate of loan may be available if you study abroad for a continuous period of eight weeks or more. An extra weekly amount (means-tested) may also be available if your course is longer than the standard 38 weeks (including Christmas and Easter holidays). Check with the body that assesses your eligibility.

Student loans in the 2003–4 academic year			
	Non-means-tested part of loan	Means-tested part [2]	Maximum loan available
Full-year loans			
London [1]	£3,695	£1,235	£4,930
Elsewhere	£3,000	£1,000	£4,000
You live at home	£2,375	£790	£3,165
Final-year loans			
London [1]	£3,205	£1,070	£4,275
Elsewhere	£2,605	£865	£3,470
You live at home	£2,070	£695	£2,765

[1] London is defined as the area covered by the City of London and the Metropolitan Police District
[2] An extra means-tested amount may be available if your course is longer than the normal academic year

Repaying the loan

You do not have to start repaying your loan until the April after you have finished your course, and then only if your salary is more than £10,000. The most you will have to repay each year will be 9 per cent of your income above £10,000.

So if you are earning £13,000, your monthly repayments will be 9 per cent of £3,000 divided by 12. Payments will be collected by the Inland Revenue either direct from your salary if you become an employee or by being added to your tax bill if you become self-employed. If your income never rises above £10,000 throughout your working life, you will not have to repay any part of the loan. If you are still repaying the loan when you reach 65, the loan will be cancelled. This will also be the case if you suffer a permanent disability or die.

Low-rate loans

Although a student loan is not an interest-free loan, it is a low-interest loan because the amount you owe is increased each year only in line with inflation. Even if you do not plan to use the entire amount of money, it is worth taking the maximum loan you are allowed and putting it in a savings account that pays interest at a higher rate than inflation.

Extra grants

As well as student loans, some students may also be entitled to grants (which do not have to be paid back). Extra grants may be available if:

- you have a disability and you incur extra costs or expenses a result of this in attending your course
- you have dependants – for example, children, or an adult relative or spouse who depends on you financially
- you are a lone parent
- you have to travel abroad as part of your course
- you were in care immediately before you started your course or you were in care at the time you finished compulsory schooling at age 16

- you are training to be a health professional
- you are training to be a teacher.

With the exception of grants for students with disabilities, all the grants mentioned above are means-tested. For more details of grants available for students with disabilities, ask for the booklet *Bridging the Gap* from the Department for Education and Skills (DfES).★ For information about other grants and bursaries, contact the body responsible for assessing your entitlement to financial support or – if you are training to be a health professional or teacher – the college where you are planning to study.

The means-test

When the body responsible for assessing you has told you that you and your chosen course are eligible for financial support, it will send you a financial form to fill in. This will ask for details of your income, and that of your parents or your spouse (if applicable). Your parents' income will not be taken account of in this means-test if you are permanently estranged from them, they cannot be traced, you are in care or you are an independent student.

If your financial circumstances – or those of your parents (or spouse) – change during the year, let your assessing body know. It may reassess your entitlement to financial help.

Help from your college

If you are eligible to take out a student loan, you may be able to get extra support once you have started at college if you find yourself in financial difficulties. Your student support or student services office should be able to tell you if you can apply for:

- **a hardship loan** up to a maximum of £250. You will get this only if you have already received the first instalment of your main student loan and you can satisfy your college that you are in financial difficulty
- **Access Funds**, which are aimed both at students who may be put off going into higher education because of the costs involved and at students who have serious financial difficulties. You must normally be eligible for a student loan and have applied for a hardship loan as well.

Student overdrafts

Student accounts differ from ordinary bank accounts because of the interest-free overdrafts they offer. When choosing one, you should ignore the gimmicky free gifts and concentrate on:

- **the size of the overdraft** The bigger the free overdraft limit the better, even if you do not intend to use it
- **what it costs for a bigger overdraft** Some banks start to charge extra if you arrange a larger overdraft than their standard limit, and all banks will charge a lot extra if you go over an agreed limit without asking first
- **running costs** There are usually no charges but it is worth checking
- **the terms after you graduate** Some banks extend the free overdraft facility for up to a year or two after graduation, which is when you are most likely to need it
- **the availability of cash machines** near to where you plan to study.

Paying grant and loan cheques into an overdrawn account

If your overdraft exceeds the bank's agreed overdraft facility, any additional funds paid in to your account will probably be used to repay your unarranged borrowing and you will not be able to draw out the same amount of money that you paid in. This may cause you to suffer severe financial hardship, particularly by the end of the term. For this reason you should always try to negotiate an increased overdraft if you think you are going to need one. If you do go over your limit you can check with your bank before paying in the funds, to find out what it will do with the money when it clears. If necessary, you could open an account with another bank or building society that will allow you to draw out all of the money that you paid in.

Getting a bank loan to clear your overdraft

If you are a student with little or no income, you should be wary about obtaining a bank loan as a way of consolidating your existing overdraft into manageable payments. There is a danger that you will find yourself faced with unaffordable repayments on both loan and overdraft.

Bank staff are often sympathetic to students in debt and will be reluctant to pressurise you into making repayments. However, where the overdraft has become unmanageable, interest may continue to be added at a high rate on the unauthorised part of the overdraft, and charges for letters and administration may continue to accrue. Rather than allow things to get this far out of hand, you should talk to your bank about the possibility of increasing your overdraft limit.

Money owed to colleges and universities

Some students find themselves in debt to their university or college because of money that they have borrowed to cover financial hardship, tuition fees, accommodation or fines. If you fail to repay these debts, the institution can take action against you, which may include forcing you to withdraw from the course or withholding your qualification until the debt has been repaid. If your institution is making these threats, it may be worth trying to persuade it to accept payment by instalments as a way of making the debt more manageable.

Accommodation charges

The majority of universities offer accommodation to students in the form of halls of residence, university-owned houses or flats, or in collaboration with private landlords. The tenancy contract is typically 12 months, with the balance usually payable in three instalments, coinciding with your grant or loan payments.

If you are having difficulty meeting the cost of student accommodation, you should negotiate with the university for deferred payment or for payment by instalments. Most universities are flexible when it comes to collecting arrears, and will be reluctant to evict you if you are having trouble paying. In these circumstances you need to review your entire finances rather than relying on deferred rent as a long-term solution.

Students and council tax

If you are a full-time student living in halls of residence or you are in private accommodation that is inhabited only by yourself or other students, you will not be liable to pay council tax. However, if you share a house or flat with non-students, who do have to pay this tax, you may have to contribute a share of the fee.

If you are being charged for council tax, you should contact the council tax offices and establish whether your council tax demand is accurate. Universities and institutions typically make lists of students available to council tax offices to help them determine whether individuals are entitled to receive a remission of the charge.

Postgraduate loans

Many banks and lending institutions make loans to students for the purpose of funding postgraduate courses such as MScs, MAs and PhDs. These loans are regulated under the Consumer Credit Act and have special terms of repayment, such as zero repayments until the completion of the course, or repayments that commence part way through the course. If you are having problems repaying the loan, you should refer to the advice given in Chapter 4.

Career development loans

Career development loans (CDLs) are interest-free loans made to qualifying applicants, to cover the costs of tuition for postgraduates or job-based training for unemployed people, for a variety of courses. The main feature of these loans is that repayment is not required for at least one month following the completion of the course, although it is demanded immediately if you drop out. This period can be extended for up to five months if you are claiming benefit.

To qualify, you must be over 18 and not be in receipt of a mandatory undergraduate grant. You can borrow between £200 and £8,000, which represents up to 80 per cent of the course fees, books and study materials (100 per cent of the fees if you have been unemployed for three months or longer). CDLs can be granted only for courses lasting for two years or less. CDLs are non-priority debts, and if you are having trouble keeping up with your payments you should refer to the strategies outlined in Chapter 4.

A free booklet on how to claim CDLs can be obtained from the Department for Education and Skills (DfES)*.

Choosing bankruptcy as a way to clear student debt

Although recent press coverage of student debt has suggested that some may be driven to consider declaring bankruptcy, it should be stressed here that there are many reasons why this is not recommended:

- in most cases you will not be able to incorporate your student loan into the bankruptcy
- you will find it a lot more difficult to get credit, even after the period of bankruptcy is over and you have been discharged
- you will be prevented from entering certain professions, such as accountancy and the law, and may appear less attractive to potential employers
- your personal possessions will be at risk if they can be sold to pay back creditors.

Unless your debts are cripplingly high, bankruptcy should not be seen as an option. Other repayment strategies that you can adopt have already been discussed in this book, and creditors are usually prepared to come to an arrangement if you are really struggling to pay them back. More information about bankruptcy is given in Chapter 6.

CHAPTER 6

Administration orders, IVAs and bankruptcy

If you have many different debts, and you are unable to reach an agreement with your creditors, it is possible to reach a solution using court procedures. You can do this via:

- an administration order
- an Individual Voluntary Arrangement (IVA)
- bankruptcy.

Administration orders

If you have at least one High Court or County Court Judgment (CCJ) against you, and your total debts are no more than £5,000, you can apply for an 'administration order' (AO). This allows the court to send payments to all your creditors. You make one monthly payment to the court and this is then split between all your creditors in a way the court decides.

Once this happens, a creditor can't take any action against you, and must stop adding interest to your debt. The administration order can include:

- consumer credit debts including credit cards
- council tax arrears
- maintenance arrears
- hire purchase arrears

- rent/mortgage arrears
- gas, electricity, phone and water bills
- court fines.

Some creditors may object to being included on the administration order, but the court can override such protests. Debts that cannot be included in the administration order are Social Fund licences and benefit overpayments.

Setting up an administration order

The application for an administration order is made on form N92. Notes on how to fill in this form are available from the court in form N270. There is no fee for making the application, although the court will deduct 10 pence in the pound from each payment that you make to cover the costs of administration. An administration order will be listed on the Register of County Court Judgment, and may affect your ability to obtain credit in the future.

After the court receives your form, it will decide whether to order a hearing. In the majority of cases, a hearing will not be necessary and the judge will make his or her decision based on your paper application.

The judge will expect the debt to be cleared within three years. If you cannot afford to make sufficiently high repayments, the judge will consider whether this period should be extended. This decision can also be made without a hearing.

If a hearing is arranged, it is vital that you attend. You may take an adviser with you if necessary.

The court hearing

Your creditors will be sent details of the administration order along with your proposed payments, and will have up to 14 days to make an objection to the granting of the order. If any objections are raised, the hearing will go ahead, otherwise the court will usually agree to implement the administration order.

At the hearing the district judge will decide on whether to grant the administration order from the information that you have already supplied to the court. It is vital that you attend the hearing. Creditors, however, rarely attend, although their presence can be useful, especially if the court needs further clarification on your financial position during the course of the hearing.

Once the administration order has been put in place, your creditors will be bound by the order and will not be able to pursue you for payment. Interest is frozen on the debts, and provided that you keep up the payments to the court, your obligations to your creditors will cease when the payments have been completed. Note that ten per cent of the payments that you make to the court will go towards court costs, and the remainder will be paid to your creditors.

How payments are made

If you are employed, the payments will usually be made by attachment of earnings, unless you request otherwise, using form N92. More information about attachment of earnings is given on pages 116–17.

If you fail to keep up payments on the order, the court will contact you and request one of the following:

- a payment to make up the arrears
- an explanation as to why you have failed to keep up with the payments
- a proposal explaining how you intend to keep up with the arrears

- a proposal from you requesting an alteration of the conditions of the order.

The district judge will decide on a course of action following your reply. Your creditors will be notified and can raise objections within 14 days. If an objection is made, a hearing will be arranged, during which time the district judge will decide on whether the administration order should be suspended, varied or cancelled.

If you do not reply to the court's request, the administration order will be cancelled within 14 days. If this happens, your creditors will be notified that the court will no longer be making payments, and that they must pursue the debt in the normal way. However, a large majority of creditors will give up trying to collect the debt at this point, because after the failure of court action, further action is unlikely to succeed.

Changing the terms of an administration order

The court will usually review the administration order periodically. If you find yourself unable to continue making your regular payments to the court because you cannot afford to do so, you should send a letter to the court explaining why you are having difficulty keeping up with your payments and enclosing a financial statement. A hearing will then be arranged for the court to consider whether to:

- reduce the payments in line with your request
- suspend the payments for a specified period of time
- make a composition order or to vary an ongoing one
- include one or more additional creditors into the administration order

● make an attachment of earnings order (see pages 116–117).

Composition orders

Where debts cannot be cleared in a 'reasonable time' (around three years) the court will often be open to a proposition called a composition order. This means that your creditors will receive a lesser sum than the actual amount owed, which may be paid by instalments.

Let's say that you owe your creditors a total of £5,000, and you have a disposable income of just £80 per month. An administration order would last for no more than three years, during which period you would pay just £2,880. If a composition order is made, it will have the effect of wiping out the £2,120 remaining balance once the three years are up.

If you want to put forward your case for a composition order, you should do so by applying on form N92, and accompany your application with a letter explaining your circumstances and why you think the composition order should be made. You may decide to consult a financial adviser if you feel that his or her assistance will help you to present a better case.

Debts shared with a partner

If you and your partner are jointly liable for a debt that is to be made a subject of an administration order, each of you must make a separate application, with the debt being divided in two and paid separately.

Individual Voluntary Arrangements (IVAs)

An Individual Voluntary Arrangement (IVA) is a legally binding arrangement between you and your creditors that allows you to settle your debts without resorting to bankruptcy.

IVAs are drawn up by qualified insolvency practitioners (usually accountants). Under an IVA, you agree to pay your creditors money as a lump sum, in instalments, or both. In return, your creditors may write off part of the debt and agree not to take court action against you or make you bankrupt. With the help of the insolvency practitioner, you may be able to negotiate a reduction of your total debt, or a longer repayment period.

Creditors usually agree to IVAs if you are prepared to pay off a large amount of the debt. So an IVA is a realistic option only if you have a sufficient amount of spare money or things you can sell to help pay off your debts.

Advantages:
- if you are a business, you can continue trading
- you do not have to face the stigma of bankruptcy and the various difficulties that come with it
- more of your income may go towards repaying your creditors than in the case of bankruptcy, where significant sums can end up being swallowed up in court costs
- the arrangement can be tailored to your own situation, as you can decide which assets to make available to creditors.

Disadvantages:
- the impact on your credit rating can be similar to that of bankruptcy

- your finances will be closely supervised by your insolvency practitioner
- your house and other assets may be at risk if your creditors decide not to exclude them
- if you fail to keep up payments, you could still be made bankrupt
- you will still be responsible for your debts unlike bankruptcy
- you have to pay the costs and fees of the IVA
- secured debts cannot be made part of the IVA agreement and will need to be paid in the normal way.

An IVA can include only unsecured debts. To begin the process, you should make a list of your unsecured creditors and the amount that you think you owe them, and make an appointment with an insolvency practitioner. Insolvency practitioners can be found in the *Yellow Pages* under 'insolvency'. They often give free initial advice, but fees can differ considerably, so it pays to shop around.

The amount you have to pay your creditors will depend on your available assets and income. The insolvency practitioner will draw up a proposal, which divides your assets and income amongst your creditors based on the amount of money that you owe each creditor. The proposal will include:

- a list of your assets and income, both current and anticipated
- assets that are being made available to your creditors under the IVA as well as those that are not
- the proposed duration of the IVA and the frequency of the payments
- details of how assets will be distributed in the event of bankruptcy
- details of how the insolvency practitioner is to be paid.

Involvement of the courts

Once the insolvency practitioner has drawn up a proposal to which you agree and have signed, it will be submitted to the County Court along with an affidavit to decide if an interim order should be made. The interim order will prevent your creditors from making you bankrupt or taking any other enforcement action.

Before an interim order can be issued, the court needs to be satisfied that you have done your best to meet your obligations and satisfy your creditors. The interim order will not come into effect if you have had a similar application declined in the last 12 months, or you are an undischarged bankrupt.

Provided you satisfy the court's conditions, the court will usually endorse the proposals and a creditors' meeting will be called.

The creditors' meeting

Your creditors will receive a copy of the insolvency practitioner's proposal and must vote on whether or not to accept it. The strength of each creditor's vote will be based on the amount of money that is owed to each, so if a creditor is owed £8,000, and your debts total £32,000, that creditor will have a 25 per cent share of the vote. For the proposal to be approved, over 75 per cent of your creditors must agree to it.

When agreement has been reached, you and your creditors will have 28 days to lodge an appeal with the court, which has the power to suspend or revoke the agreement or call another creditors' meeting. It is unusual for this to happen if agreement has already been reached. Following approval, the agreement becomes binding on all the creditors who were notified of the creditors' meeting.

When the proposal has been accepted, a supervisor is appointed to manage the sale of your assets that are included in the agreement. As long as you continue to make the required payments to the supervisor, there should be no problems, but if you fail to do this the supervisor or your other creditors will usually petition for your bankruptcy. If your situation changes during the time that the IVA is in operation and you want to modify the agreement, you will need to gain the approval of the supervisor.

When the IVA has been set up, your name will be entered into a public register and held there for two years after the IVA has been completed or terminated. To check if your name is on the register, you can write to the Insolvency Service*.

Bankruptcy

Bankruptcy releases you from your debts after two or three years. By becoming bankrupt, most or all of your debt will be wiped out and creditors will have to accept that you no longer owe them money. However, your finances will be officially investigated, and you will have to make reasonable payments to your creditors for the first two or three years, if you can afford to do so.

Always seek expert advice

Bankruptcy is not an easy option and needs careful consideration. It is essential to get expert advice before applying to make yourself bankrupt.

Bankruptcy may not be suitable for people:

- with certain types of job (for example, if you work in finance, you are a solicitor, or self-employed)

- if you own (or are buying) your own home, or
- if you have a lot of other assets.

You will still have to pay the following:

- magistrates' fines
- maintenance for a partner or children
- debts from fraud, and
- some forms of student loans.

You must pay a court fee of £140 to make yourself bankrupt (even if you are receiving benefits). This fee alone can rule out bankruptcy for many people.

Advantages:

- bankruptcy can give you freedom from the stress of uncontrollable debt and enable you to make a fresh start
- you will be able to keep the money that you earn instead of paying it to your creditors. Many people, before declaring bankruptcy, are paying in excess of £1,000 a month in creditor repayments alone. Being able to keep this money can make a significant difference.

Disadvantages:

- bankruptcy will mean that you will lose any assets of real value. During the bankruptcy process, the Official Receiver will scrutinise your assets, and decide which ones should be sold to meet court costs and the demands of creditors
- during bankruptcy, you will not be able start a business with a different trading name. Starting a new business afterwards will also be a lot more difficult than it would otherwise
- secured creditors will still be able to recover any assets secured under a credit agreement
- during the period in which you are bankrupt, you will not be able to obtain credit of more than £250. In

addition, it may remain extremely difficult for you to obtain credit even after discharge

- you will be expected to declare any windfalls or assets that come into your hands while you are bankrupt
- the process can be very expensive. Much of the money raised by the sale of your assets may be swallowed up in administration costs
- during and after bankruptcy you will be prevented from holding certain offices, such as a solicitor, accountant or judge. Future employment may also be threatened and you cannot hold the post of company director
- if you have recently settled in the UK, bankruptcy could affect your right to hold British citizenship or prevent you from gaining immigration status.

Bankruptcy is for a period of three years for debts up to and exceeding £20,000. If it is a first bankruptcy, discharge will be automatic after this period. This is the standard arrangement unless you ask the court to make an order for 'summary administration'.

Summary administration

You may apply for summary administration if you owe less than £20,000 and you are able to provide the court with at least £2,000 worth of assets. The court will only recognise summary administration if you petition yourself. The principal benefit of summary administration is that the period of bankruptcy is reduced to only two years.

Deciding to go bankrupt

If you have come to the conclusion that bankruptcy is the best choice, you can petition yourself to go bankrupt. You must pay a fee (currently £140 plus a deposit of £250 towards the cost of administering your own bankruptcy).

In order to petition for bankruptcy, you should get the following forms, free of charge, from a County Court which deals with bankruptcy: you can also print forms from the Insolvency Service website★.

- **The petition** (Insolvency Rule form 6.27) – this is your request to be made bankrupt and includes the reasons for your request.
- **The statement of affairs** (Insolvency Rule form 6.28) – this form asks you to show all your assets (anything that belongs to you that may be used to pay your debts), and all your debts, including the names and addresses of the creditors and the amount you owe to each one. It contains a declaration of insolvency, which you will need to swear on oath before an officer of the court or a solicitor.

When you have completed the forms and handed them into the court along with your fee, a hearing is arranged, usually on the same day. The court will then decide whether to make an IVA or bankruptcy order, or to dismiss, adjourn or stay (suspend) proceedings.

The matter may be handed to an insolvency practitioner to arrange an IVA (see pages 90–3) if:

- your debts are below £20,000
- your assets are at least £2,000
- you have not been subject to bankruptcy proceedings in the last five years
- it seems appropriate.

Being made bankrupt by a creditor

A creditor can petition to make you bankrupt if the sum owed exceeds £750. Creditors can also club together to bring an action if the sum owed to them jointly exceeds this figure. If your creditor succeeds in making you bankrupt, you will be spared the fee which would become payable if you decided to petition yourself.

Before a creditor can apply to make you bankrupt, he or she must either have attempted to collect the debt using bailiffs, or have issued you with a statutory demand. This is a formal demand for payment, which calls for you to do one of the following:

- pay off the debt
- negotiate payment by instalments
- offer to have the debt secured against your property.

The creditor can ask for a bankruptcy hearing 21 days after the statutory demand is issued. However, you may apply to the court to have the hearing 'set aside' using forms 6.4 (application) and 6.5 (affidavit).

The bankruptcy hearing may be set aside if:

- there is doubt over the sum owed
- there is a counterclaim of more money than is owed
- the demand was issued in error – for example, the sum owed is less than £750
- you can demonstrate that you are not insolvent
- your creditor holds security that exceeds the value of the debt
- an instalment plan, which you have set up with your creditor, is being complied with.

It is worth noting that your creditor is not obliged to accept any offer below what is actually owed, however reasonable, although the court may intervene to suggest options for resolving the matter without resorting to bankruptcy.

If the statutory demand is not complied with, and is not set aside, your creditor can proceed with his or her petition for bankruptcy. It is sometimes difficult to judge the intent of a creditor and whether or not he or she is determined to make good the threat. Some unsecured creditors will use the threat of bankruptcy with little intention of taking action, as the eventual return on the debt to them is likely to be minimal.

Creditors who are personally affected by your inability to pay may seek to make you bankrupt as revenge for the loss of their money. If the notice to make you bankrupt is served on you personally, this may also demonstrate the creditor's intent. It may well be worth your while contacting your creditor and asking him what his ultimate aim is after the issue of the statutory demand.

If you sense that the creditor is serious about following through with his or her threat to make you bankrupt, there are several measures that you can take to prevent it:

- make the creditor a payment to reduce the debt to below £750
- negotiate alternative methods of repayment (see the strategies in Chapter 4)
- offer the creditor a reduced sum as a full and final offer, say between 25 and 50 per cent of the amount owed. The creditor may agree to this because he or she is unlikely to recoup such a sum if he or she follows through with the action
- consider taking out an IVA, which will allow your assets to be divided equally between your creditors.

The bankruptcy hearing

At the hearing the court will decide on whether the bankruptcy should go through in the light of the information provided in the petition. The court will need to be satisfied that you have not attempted to omit or falsify information, or to hide assets that would have a material bearing on the outcome of the decision. In making this decision, the court will consider whether:

- you have the means to repay your creditors
- an appeal has been made, or judgment has been stayed
- you have a claim against a creditor who is bringing a petition against you
- you have a counterclaim that would reduce the debt to below £750.

The court will not usually block a petition unless your income is such that it would be fair and reasonable for you to pay back your creditors within a reasonable period. In this event, the court may insist that you set up an IVA or come to another arrangement with your creditors.

Your financial affairs during bankruptcy

Your financial affairs immediately before and during bankruptcy will be managed by the Official Receiver, who is an officer appointed by the court, or an insolvency practitioner (usually an accountant). The person appointed will become your trustee during bankruptcy. If your debts exceed £20,000 and a request for summary administration is not made, the trustee will contact your creditors to decide if a meeting is to be called. It may not be in the interests of creditors to attend the meeting, and as a rule the majority of creditors will not turn up. During the meeting the creditors in attendance will be able to have a say in how your assets are divided.

The trustee will attempt to secure as much money as possible for your creditors. He or she will investigate your affairs to find evidence of criminal wrongdoing such as concealment of assets, and has the power to contact a large number of organisations and institutions in order to obtain details of assets or liabilities that you might still be holding. In addition to this, notice of your bankruptcy will be given to local authorities, courts, bailiffs, utility suppliers, the Land Registry and other professional bodies. During your bankruptcy, you will not be allowed to obtain credit over £250. In addition you will not be able to sell anything or realise any money without informing the trustee; failure to do so could lead to a fine and/or imprisonment. The trustee also has powers to redirect mail if appropriate or make an order for you to attend court under oath, although this is very seldom done.

If you are not happy about the way in which your affairs have been managed, you can complain to the insolvency practitioner's professional body which will take up your complaint with the practitioner concerned.

Yellow Pages has details of practitioners in your area, or you can search the website www.ipa.uk.com. This site contains additional information about the services offered as well as links to other sites.

Sale of goods

The trustee will create a plan which allows for your goods to be sold, and may visit you at your home to see that this is carried out. A visit is compulsory at a business premises.

You can keep some goods if you become bankrupt:

- **tools of the trade, including a vehicle** Although you will probably be allowed to keep a car valued at below

£1,000 if you need it for work, a higher-value vehicle may have to be traded in so that you can purchase a cheaper model

- **household goods necessary for basic living** The courts are quite lenient when it comes to deciding what can be taken. Most fixtures and fittings, particularly those that form a part of your property may be left, along with low-value, resaleable goods. Although luxury goods such as video cameras or expensive hi-fi systems will be taken by the court, the rules are usually less stringent than the rules followed by bailiffs (see Chapter 8).

Jointly owned assets

Any assets that you jointly own with someone else, but which can legitimately be seized by the court because of their value, may be sold and the proceeds shared equally between your creditors and the joint-owner of the asset. As an alternative to this, the joint-owner can agree to buy out your share and hand the money to the trustee.

Pension rights

Whether you can keep your pension will depend on whether it has started to be paid and the date on which you declared bankruptcy. Whatever the date of your bankruptcy, if you are already receiving a pension, some or all of this income can be claimed to pay to your creditors.

If your pension has not yet started and you became bankrupt prior to the 29 May 2000, the trustee was able to seize most of any pension fund you had built up in a personal pension or retirement annuity contract for the benefit of your creditors, but usually not any rights you had built up in an occupational scheme. However, any rights you built up due to being 'contracted out' of the state pension scheme could not be seized. If your bankruptcy takes place on or after 29 May 2000, in general the trustee will have no power to seize any of the money in your pension fund, and you will be able to keep all of the money and benefits that have already accrued. However, the trustee can claim against your pension rights if your contributions are deemed to be 'excessive', so you cannot protect your assets from creditors simply by diverting as much as possible into your pension arrangement.

If you have a pension it would be wise to seek professional advice.

Bank accounts

Before you are made bankrupt the trustee will close down any bank accounts that you own and confiscate any money in them, which will be used to pay back your creditors. You may apply to the trustee for a modest sum to be returned to cover essential household expenses such as food and heating.

It is important to make sure that you have enough money to cover the expenses that will inevitably arise after bankruptcy. For this reason it's better to use your remaining funds to pay back arrears that may have built up on secured loans such as mortgage payments, court fines and utility bills as these will not be wiped out after you are made bankrupt. It would be wise to make these payments some time before actually becoming bankrupt to avoid giving the impression that you are concealing assets from your other creditors.

During and after bankruptcy, you will have to apply to the trustee before opening a new account, and the trustee will keep a close eye on any accounts that you do hold in case savings become available that could be paid to creditors. Although most banks will not let you open a new account while you are bankrupt, there are some that do (see pages 176–7.).

Property and bankruptcy

You will usually be allowed to keep your home if its sale will not release any value, but if you do so the court will register a charging order on the property, which means that it may be sold at a later date if it increases in value substantially. This can be the case even after discharge which means that if you were to sell your home, any profit will go to the trustee to pay your debts.

When making the decision about whether or not your home should be sold, the court may consider the following:

- the interests of your creditors
- whether or not your spouse contributed to your bankruptcy
- the needs and resources of your children and spouse
- other relevant circumstances.

If you share your property with your spouse and only one of you is being made bankrupt, the trustee will normally ask you or your spouse to purchase the other half of the property. The Insolvency Act 1986 makes it possible for the property to be sold by the trustee if the other partner is not willing to make this purchase. If you have young children living at home, a sale may not be demanded for at least a year to allow you and your family to resettle.

Protecting your home

If keeping your home is your main priority, there are a number of ways in which you can protect it from being sold or repossessed if you become bankrupt.

- **Do not overstate the value of your property** When petitioning yourself for bankruptcy, you will have to state the value of your property and the amount of money that is secured on it, so that the court can determine the amount of equity in the property. If there is a large amount of equity in the property, the court may order you to sell your home for the benefit of your creditors, so for this reason it is important to seek a valuation that does not overstate the value of your home.

Just because you have equity in your property does not necessarily mean that the court will automatically order its sale. The trustee will consider other factors such as the needs of the persons residing there, the value of the property and the interests of your creditors.

- **Encourage your partner/parent/friend to buy out your interest in the property** The trustee will give a third party such as a spouse, friend or relative the option of purchasing your share of the equity at the time of your bankruptcy. This avoids the need to make a charging order on the property (see pages 117–19). If you decide to take advantage of this option, your third party will have to pay the court the amount of equity present at the time of the bankruptcy, less the sale costs that would arise. If there is little or no equity, or the cost of selling of the property would be greater than the value raised from its sale, a nominal sum of £1 would need to be paid to the trustee plus costs (currently £211).

  Getting a third party to buy your share of the trustee's interest in the property can be a wise move because if house prices rise and the balance on your mortgage steadily reduces as you continue to meet your mortgage payments, the equity in your home will increase over time. If you decide to take this option, it is recommended that you to speak to a solicitor first, especially if you have a second mortgage.

- **Keep up to date with mortgage payments** If you have kept up your mortgage payments or you are not in serious arrears, your mortgage company will not want to repossess your home provided that you continue to keep up payments. The company will continue to hold your home as security, even after bankruptcy.

Hire purchase goods

Hire purchase goods remain your responsibility after bankruptcy. If you keep up payments, the goods will remain in your possession unless their value is significantly higher than the money that you owe, in which case the trustee may order them to be sold.

Disposal of assets

If you sell or dispose of assets after you have become bankrupt, or you did this during the time when you were technically insolvent, the trustee can order the sale to be set aside so that your creditors may benefit from the sale of the asset.

The trustee may take action if he or she believes that you have acted fraudulently by protecting assets that would otherwise have had to be sold to pay back creditors in bankruptcy.

Windfalls during bankruptcy

If you manage to accrue a sizeable sum of money during your period of bankruptcy, the trustee will use this money to pay your creditors. If you become the beneficiary of a will, this money will also go to pay your creditors unless you see to it that the money is left to a close friend or family member so that you will not lose your share.

Cancellation of a bankruptcy order

A bankruptcy order may be annulled or cancelled at any time provided you have met all financial obligations to your creditors, or there was a valid reason why the petition should not have gone through in the first place.

Changes in the law that will affect bankruptcy

Recently, the government announced sweeping changes in the law relating to bankruptcy. The Enterprise Act, the relevant part of which is expected to come into force in 2004, is designed to help you get back on your feet more quickly, by creating an automatic discharge within one year instead of three, and also includes the following changes:

- the abolition of summary administration
- abandoning the exclusions currently in place that prevent you from holding certain offices (such as magistrate)
- failure to keep proper accounts or gambling debts will no longer be considered bankruptcy offences.

Some of the restrictions will still apply while the bankruptcy is in place, namely the inability to hold the position of company director, not being able to obtain credit above £250, and trading in another name other than the one under which you were made bankrupt. In instances where the court considers you have acted dishonestly, the Official Receiver can place restrictions on you for between 2 and 15 years.

Discharge from bankruptcy

In ordinary bankruptcies, at the time of writing discharge is automatic after three years (or two years if the order is made under summary administration). However, if the court decides that you have not acted lawfully when meeting your obligations to your creditors, it may call a hearing and suspend your automatic right to discharge, asking you to reapply for discharge at a later date.

In the case of criminal bankruptcy, a court order will be required before discharge. This will be not less than five years following the bankruptcy.

Debts after discharge

After discharge, the court will issue you with a certificate. All debts incurred before bankruptcy will now become unenforceable except for the following:

- debts to secured creditors (excepting any amounts owing on secured assets that were sold)
- debts obtained fraudulently
- maintenance orders
- personal injury claims
- fines
- family court orders
- student loans made under the Student Loans Act 1990
- debts arising from certain criminal court orders.

CHAPTER 7

Creditors and the courts

If you do not succeed in re-negotiating your repayments, fail to keep to your new repayment plan or do not act in time, your creditor may take court action. The costs of court action, and maybe legal fees, will add further to your debt. Court action may also lead to you having a County Court Judgment (CCJ) registered against you. This would go on your credit file, affect your credit rating and make it more difficult for you to get a loan or credit in the future.

However, there should be plenty of opportunities during the court process for you to agree an out-of-court settlement with the creditor and thereby avoid having a CCJ registered against you.

Court action does not necessarily mean that you will have to go to court because many of the steps in court procedures happen by post. If you are faced with court action, if you have not already done so you should seek advice from a debt counselling service – see the organisations on pages 28–9. You will be given advice on how to fill in all the forms and, if you eventually have to go to court, help presenting your case.

Impending court action

Normally, before court action is started, the creditor will send you a formal written request for the money you owe (known as a letter before action or default notice). This will probably set out details of how much you owe and how far you have fallen behind with payments. You will also be told what action the creditor intends to take if you fail to pay. This may include passing the account to a collection agency or solicitor, or taking you to court.

When you receive a notice like this, you usually have a minimum of seven days to respond, after which time the creditor is entitled to commence proceedings against you in the County Court. Failure to respond to the notice may also give the creditor the right to terminate any credit agreement, if the right did not already exist.

Receiving a claim form

In most cases, apart from mortgage and rent arrears (see Chapter 3), court action starts when the creditor (the 'claimant') asks the court to send a 'claim form' to you (the 'defendant').

The court will issue you with a claim form (form N1), which states the amount the claimant says you owe and any other amounts that the claimant expects to recover, such as court costs, solicitor's costs and interest charges. Four additional forms should accompany the claim form. These are as follows:

1. A response pack (form N9), which gives details about the forms that you need to sign and an indication to the court about what action you intend taking
2. An admission form (N9A), which should be completed if you admit the claim and you want more time to pay
3. A form for disputing the claim (N9B), which you should complete if you dispute some or all of the amount that the creditor is claiming
4. Information about how to go about completing the claim forms (N9C).

Your options

At this stage, you have two choices:

Defending the claim

You can choose to defend the claim in only a few situations:

- if you have already paid the money
- possibly if the creditor has already agreed to allow you to make lower payments, or
- possibly if the creditor has refused to discuss your offer of lower payments.

Don't defend a claim without getting expert advice first. If you lose your case, you may have to pay the creditor's court costs, which would mean that your debt might become much bigger.

If you aren't going to defend the claim, you might want to ask the County Court not to make you pay any court costs. This is up to the judge. He or she will decide this, taking into account if the creditor has behaved badly towards you, for example, or hasn't followed the proper procedure in getting the money you owe.

Admitting the claim

If you admit the claim, you should come up with a payment plan, based on what you think you can realistically afford.

Give special consideration to the way in which you complete form N9A, because based on the information that you supply, the court may ask you to pay the creditor back more than you can reasonably afford. Tips on how to complete some of the most important parts of form N9A are given below.

- In the employment section you will be expected to provide details of any income you are currently earning. If all or part of your income comes from being self-employed be realistic about the amount of income you get, particularly if it is sporadic. Overestimating figures like this could prove to be problematic because the creditor will expect to receive more money back.

- Cash savings are taken into account by the court only if they exceed one-and-a-half times your income. If you do have more than this amount, it is important that you use this money to pay off any arrears that you may have to priority creditors, or the court will judge that you are in a position to repay your unsecured creditor with the money in the account.

- In the expenses section, make sure you include all of your regular outgoings and priority commitments, even if you have fallen behind on payments. Legitimate expenses will be deducted by the court from the amount you have left to pay your creditor.

- In the section that asks you about priority debts, make sure that you mention any arrears that you have with your priority creditors or make arrangements with them to clear the arrears beforehand.

- In the credit debts section, mention any unsecured debts that you are currently paying, and add an extra sheet if you are unable to fit all of your unsecured creditors on.

- In the offer of payment box, you should be prepared to make the court an offer of payment, even if it is only £1 a month. The court will be likely to accept this offer if you are able to demonstrate that you are unable to pay any more.

If the creditor accepts this offer, it will be recorded by the court and you will have to stick to it. But if the creditor turns down your offer, then usually a court official will consider what you have offered and what the creditor wants, then decide how much you should pay (though there is no hearing in court).

In these circumstances, when deciding how much you should pay, the court uses a formula or calculator. This measures your disposable income by deducting items such as living costs, payments to priority and non-priority creditors, and court debts, from your income and savings. When a figure is reached, the court will normally do one of the following:

- if your disposable income is greater than the creditor's demand, the court will insist that you meet the instalment repayments in full
- if your disposable income is less than the creditor's demand for instalments, the court will ask you to pay all of your disposable income to your creditor
- if the means-test shows that you have zero or negative disposable income, the matter will be passed to an adjudicator who will make a decision based on your circumstances. You may still be asked to make a contribution.

If you don't agree, or the creditor doesn't agree, with the court's payment plan, you have 14 days to ask for the decision to be 'redetermined' by a district judge. If the court then decides to have a hearing, the case will be transferred to your nearest court. You and the creditor will both be able to have a say before the court decides whether to change the payment plan in the original judgment.

After this stage, how much you should pay can't normally be varied. If you don't make the payments described in the judgment, you may have to pay interest on the money you owe.

If you do not respond to a claim

If you receive a claim form, do not ignore it. If you don't respond to a claim at all, it doesn't just go away. The procedure will continue and the court will come up with a judgment, which will include how much you should pay. If you don't make these payments, the creditor can legally use bailiffs or other measures to get the money you owe. If you have not already done so, get outside help from the organisations listed on pages 28–9.

However, there are circumstances where you might not have been able to respond to the claim (for example, because it was sent to the wrong address, or you were away when it was sent). If this is so, you may be able to get the judgment set aside. To do so, though, you will usually have to show that you have a good chance of defending the claim or you have another good reason for it to be set aside. If you want to get a claim set aside, you should first get expert advice.

If you can no longer afford the payments

If something has changed which means you can no longer afford the repayments set by the court, you may be able to apply to have your payments reduced. But you need a good reason – for example, you lose your job, or your family grows.

Exemptions from payment

If your financial situation means that you really won't be able to repay the debt, or you are in a genuine crisis (for example, you have a serious illness), the court may be able to vary or suspend ('stay') the judgment, so that you end up paying smaller instalments or nothing for the moment.

If you are asking to pay smaller instalments, remember that the court will expect you to make a sensible offer towards the payments, even if you can offer only a nominal amount. The court will determine if your offer is suitable by using a formula or calculator.

If you apply for a general stay, you need to bear in mind that court costs will be added to the debt that you may have to pay after the stay has been lifted. The court will be more likely to agree to a suspension if there is a good reason, for example, you are a single parent on Income Support looking after young children or you are sick or have a disability.

Both applications are made to the court by filling in form N244, which you can get from the County Court. There is a £25 fee for making the application, although you can apply for remission of this by completing form EX160. You should also accompany this form with:

- a financial statement of your affairs
- an explanation of how you will be adversely affected by the paying of the court fees
- other reasons in support of your application.

For more information, see the Court Service's leaflet *I Cannot Pay My Judgment – What do I do?* available from County Courts.

If you don't make the payments

If you do not pay what has been ordered in a judgment, the creditor can ask the court to take various steps to make you pay. This is known as 'enforcing judgment'. The main steps, and what they mean for you, are set out below.

Warrant of execution

If you fail to keep to the payments ordered by the court, the court may issue a warrant of execution, which will give the creditor the right to appoint a bailiff to seize your goods.

Applying for a warrant of execution continues to be a creditor's most used means of recovering payment, and in the year 2000, courts in the UK authorised over 470,000 warrants. For more details see Chapter 8.

Attachment of earnings

This is when the creditor asks the court to make an order to take regular payments from your wages. The court will notify you that an application for an attachment of earnings order has been made on form N55. Another form N56 will also be enclosed asking you for certain details and requiring you to complete a statement of means, which should be returned to the court.

If you don't co-operate with the court in this, you could be arrested or sent to prison for up to 14 days. The court also has the power to contact your employer and order it to declare your earnings. You can prevent the attachment of earnings order from going ahead by agreeing to make the required payments to the court, and by completing the required section on form N56. However, if you fail to keep up with the payments, the court has the power to proceed with the attachment of earnings order.

If there is an attachment of earnings, the court will set a 'protected earnings rate' (PER). This is a level below which deductions cannot be made. It is based on Income Support rates, and takes account of other earnings (such as your partner's wages) and things you must pay for. The court will then set a normal deduction rate (NDR), which is normally less than half of the income you have left after the PER is taken from your wages or salary.

A fee of £1 is imposed on each deduction. In addition, if you leave your job and/or become unemployed, you will have to notify the court within seven days or the court may impose a fine. If you become unemployed, you should write to inform the court of this change immediately.

If the court is imposing an attachment of earnings order and you already have one running, you can apply to the court to combine the two. This should be done on form N244. There are no limits to the amount of orders that can be combined – you may find it more convenient to make one larger monthly payment this way, rather than several individual payments.

Charging order

A charging order is when the creditor asks the court to secure the debt to your home. The effect of a charging order is that the debt will be secured against your property and an entry made on the Land Registry. This means that when your house is sold, the creditor will be repaid from the proceeds of the sale.

There are two stages in the charging order process:

1. Interim charging order

This is where the creditor makes an application to the County Court for the debt to be secured against your property in order that the creditor may gain from the proceeds if the property is sold at a later date. This will have the effect of turning the unsecured debt into a secured one.

The creditor will have to prove that you are in arrears with your payments and that you are the owner of your property. The creditor will also have to send the court details of your other creditors, if known, so as to give them the opportunity to object to the granting of the charging order.

If your other creditors raise no objections, the creditor lodging the charging order will be able to apply to the Land Registry for a 'caution'. This means that if you attempt to sell your property, the creditor will be informed of your action and will be given the opportunity to object to the sale. If the sale goes ahead, the creditor will be paid out of the proceeds.

An interim charging order can also be lodged against shares or other valuable assets that you own. This will prevent their sale or the payment of dividends from them while the charging order is in force.

2. Final charging order

When the interim order has been granted, the creditor will be able to decide whether to apply to make the charging order final. This will give the creditor the right to ask the court to order a sale of the property if the conditions for the repayment of the debt have not been met.

The court will make the decision to make a charging order final based on your ability to pay the creditor back and whether your other creditors will agree to the final charging order going ahead. You will be given the opportunity to object to the order being made final, and if you do proceedings will be transferred to your local court.

You can help to prevent the interim charging order from being made final by:

- making sure all of the required instalment payments due under the judgment have been paid to date. If they have all been paid, the court cannot agree to the order
- explaining your personal circumstances; if you are old, ill or very vulnerable, the judge is more likely to be sympathetic to your case

- showing that the imposition of the charging order prejudices the rights of your other creditors because there is insufficient equity in your property to meet all of your unsecured debts
- showing that other measures are more appropriate than imposing the charging order – such as a new instalment order
- explaining that your situation seems likely to improve in the near future, and you will be able to recommence making payments to your creditor.

It is rare for a court to order the sale of a property which is the subject of a charging order. In the unusual cases where a sale has been ordered, any conditions attached to the charging order are likely not to have been met. Even when this is the case, the court will use its discretion to decide whether or not to enforce the sale.

Third-party debt order

A third-party debt order is usually made to stop a defendant taking money out of his or her bank or building society account. Money owed to a creditor is then paid from the account.

As a first step, the creditor obtains a court order freezing the relevant account. If the judge is satisfied with the information the creditor has provided, the judge will make an interim third-party debt order. A copy will be sent to the creditor and the third-party bank or building society, say. A copy is not sent to the debtor until seven days after it has been sent to the third party. This is to ensure that the third party 'freezes' the money before the debtor becomes aware of the order.

A hearing will then be arranged, during which the court will have to decide whether or not to make the order final, in which case the third party will be instructed to meet the creditor's demands from that account.

If you are dependent on the money in the third-party account, you should attend the hearing to tell the court why you need the money. The court is more likely to overturn the interim order or make you a 'hardship payment order' if you can convince it that you are suffering from real financial hardship, or that you need the money to pay pressing priority creditors. It is important that you provide documentary evidence to back your claim, such as a financial statement.

High Court enforcement

For some types of debt over £600, and debt on unregulated agreements, your creditor could use High Court Sheriffs' Officers acting as bailiffs to collect the debt. If you cannot come to an agreement on how much you should pay, you will need to get advice on applying to the court to stop this bailiff action, and arranging a way to pay what you can afford.

Bankruptcy

If the amount you owe is more than £750, the creditor can also apply to make you bankrupt. For more details see pages 93–107.

Information orders

After getting a judgment, the creditor can ask the court to order you to be questioned in court about your circumstances, in order to find out how best to get the money you owe. The creditor asks for an Order to Obtain Information from a Judgment Debtor. Although not a method of enforcing judgment, this is a way in which a creditor can get more information about your finances.

The court will send you a questionnaire and affidavit (statement under oath), asking you to provide details of your income, goods and other assets. On the basis of the information that you have supplied, the court may order you to attend a hearing to gather more information about your means.

If the court decides to go ahead with the hearing, you will be expected to bring along supporting documents including outstanding bills, pay slips, rent book, Income Support receipts etc. Attendance costs may be claimed back from the court.

In court, you can be ordered to answer questions on oath, about:

- your income
- what you spend money on
- what you own.

If you do not attend the hearing, the court could issue a warrant for your arrest. However, the creditor may call off the hearing if you provide it with the details it requires.

Once the information order has been completed, the information is forwarded to the creditor, who will be able to decide on the best strategy for recovering money – for example, by attachment of earnings or bailiff action.

Appeals

It is possible to appeal against a court decision about enforcement. However, grounds for appeal can be quite limited and the costs considerable. You should therefore take legal advice from a solicitor before considering such action.

County Court Judgments

If a creditor gets a 'money-only' claim, you will have a County Court Judgment (CCJ) registered against you. This will go on your credit file, affect your credit rating and probably make it more difficult for you to get a loan or credit card in the future. It will also increase the amount you owe, because you will have to pay the creditor's costs awarded against you.

However, there are advantages to a CCJ if you really can't come to an agreement with the creditor to pay back the money. It should mean that the creditor stops adding interest to what you owe and, in most cases, the court will set a repayment plan that you should be able to afford. As long as you stick to the plan ordered by the court, the creditor can't use methods of enforcement, such as bailiffs, against you.

Time orders

Most loans are what are called 'regulated' credit agreements. This is because, if you fail to reach a suitable agreement with your creditor, there are ways through the courts that you can make an arrangement to pay back the loan at a rate based on what you can afford.

If you have a second mortgage (or a loan secured on your home, regulated by the Consumer Credit Act 1974) and your payment plan is refused by the lender, you may be able to obtain a time order.

A time order can reduce or even stop the interest that is adding up on the money you owe, and reduce the instalments you pay to a level you can afford. But you have to show the court that you have real difficulty making the payments. You may also have to show that you would be able to pay the full instalments again at a later time. An example would be if you took out a second mortgage for home improvements, but were unable to continue making the payments halfway through the loan because of illness or injury. You could therefore propose to reduce payments by half for the next six months while you are recovering, and go back to making full payments when you return to work.

Other grounds for a time order might be if the reason for your taking out the loan was the result of overzealous selling on behalf of the lender, or the terms of the agreement were onerous.

- If you are applying for a time order in response to a summons for possession, you must complete form N244 and accompany this form with an affidavit. A fee of £80 will be required, but an exemption of the fee can be applied for on form Ex160 if you are on benefits or on a very low income.

Time orders may be amended at any time at the request of either the lender or the borrower. A good example of where the court might act to amend the order is if your circumstances change during the period that the time order is in operation.

CHAPTER 8

Bailiffs and imprisonment

Bailiffs

Bailiffs are used by most types of creditor. It is a common tactic to threaten to send in the bailiffs to take things you own, which the creditor can sell to repay your debt.

If you are in debt, the threat of bailiffs coming into your house and seizing your valuable possessions can be daunting. However, you aren't powerless. Despite the impression that bailiffs may give you, in most cases they are not allowed to force their way into your home.

Debt collectors

It's important to realise that debt collectors are not the same as bailiffs. Debt collectors have no legal rights to take any action against you, apart from asking you to pay. If you believe a debt collector is falsely acting as a bailiff, contact the trading standards department at your local council. If you are being threatened, contact the police.

Court powers granted to bailiffs

Both the County Court and the magistrates' court use bailiffs to collect outstanding debts. Bailiffs are most commonly used to collect arrears of council tax and community charge, but are also used to collect unpaid income tax and unpaid fines as well as other types of debt.

Bailiffs are often used to enforce payment of County Court Judgments (CCJs). If you have a CCJ and you don't make the payments, the court may issue a 'warrant of execution' which gives the bailiffs power to act.

County Court bailiffs also carry out evictions after possession proceedings (see 'Possession proceedings (for mortgage or rent arrears)', page 37). In this situation you do not have any right to stop them coming into your home.

Bailiffs usually become involved in the following way.

1. The court sends you a letter, telling you about the intended course of action if you fail to pay the outstanding balance or come to another acceptable arrangement.
2. The court issues a warrant of execution to the bailiff.
3. The bailiff delivers you a warning notice telling you that action will be taken if you fail to make payment within seven days.
4. The bailiff begins taking action for distress.

You can, however, stop this process by offering to make a payment of some kind and filling in a special form (N245) at your local County Court, giving a statement about what you can afford.

Preventing bailiff action
You will need to apply immediately in order to give the court time to consider your circumstances.

Your application to the court should contain an offer of payment, even if it is only a nominal amount (50 pence a month is usually accepted if the court accepts your explanation of hardship). You should also explain why bailiff action would not work – for example, your possessions aren't worth very much, or you rely on your car or home computer for your income.

If you have no income and are unable to make any payments, or you have no goods of value, you should ask the creditor to write the debt off (see pages 67–8).

The court will send your offer of payment to the creditor who will have up to 14 days to object to your offer. If no objection is made, the court will go ahead with your offer. If an objection is made, the court will use the determination of means calculator to decide if you can pay any more, or send the case to an adjudicating officer.

The court can send in the bailiffs if you fail to come to an acceptable arrangement.

Bailiffs' rights of entry

It is vital that you understand bailiffs' rights of entry because you have certain powers to prevent them from seizing your valuable possessions. The most important thing to remember is that bailiffs have no automatic right to enter your home, and if you refuse to let them in, they must respect your decision and leave.

If you do let a bailiff into your home, he or she will not generally seize property on the first visit but will ask you to sign a walking possession order. This asks you to pay a flat fee (normally £10) which allows you to keep possession of your goods, while recognising the right of the bailiff to return to remove them.

If the bailiffs have been unable to seize your goods because they couldn't gain access or you have no goods, they will pass the debt back to the council. If this happens, you should resume negotiations with the council immediately because the next step may be an attachment of earnings order (see pages 116–17) or imprisonment (see pages 133–4).

Contact your local Citizens Advice Bureau (CAB)★ or your local councillor if you are unable to meet the council's demands for payment. They may be able to initiate negotiations on your behalf.

Goods exempt from seizure

The general rule is that bailiffs are permitted to seize goods from a debtor to the value of the debt, and in practice most bailiffs will attempt to seize any goods which are likely to realise sufficient value on sale to cover the debt. However, there are a number of goods that bailiffs are not allowed to seize, and if they attempt to do so you have the right to demand that the goods remain in your possession. The following is a list of goods that are exempt from bailiff seizure:

- goods that are hired or subject to hire purchase agreements (goods on finance or credit agreements are not exempt however)
- clothing reasonably required for the use of the debtor or any member of the debtor's household
- fixtures and fittings that form part of the property itself. Examples include light fittings, kitchen units and shelf units
- goods owned by third parties. However, many bailiffs will attempt to seize any goods initially, regardless of their ownership, unless title can clearly be proved afterwards by means of a receipt of purchase
- implements, tools of trade, books or other equipment including a car or van reasonably required for the use of the debtor or any member of the debtor's household in the pursuit of trade or business (not exceeding £1,000)
- medical aids or medical equipment reasonably required for the use of the debtor or any member of his or her household

- books or other articles, including a computer, reasonably required for the education or training of the debtor or any member of the debtor's household (not exceeding £1,000)
- toys for the use of any child who is a member of the debtor's household
- articles reasonably required for the care or upbringing of a child who is a member of the debtor's household.

The following goods are also exempt if they serve a basic purpose, and are reasonably required for the use of the person residing there or another member of the household:

- linen and bedding
- tables and chairs
- food
- lighting or light fittings
- heating appliances
- curtains
- floor coverings
- furniture
- equipment or utensils used for cooking, storing or eating food
- refrigerators
- articles used for cleaning the home
- furniture used for storing clothing
- pots and pans.

Also exempt from seizure are goods that are valued at less than £50 or 10 per cent of the value of the debt, whichever is the greater. In addition, if the value of your goods is not sufficient to cover the bailiff's costs, they may not be seized.

A bailiff can't take walking possession of items inside your home if he or she has not been admitted. However, things not inside your house (a car, for example) can be taken.

Cars

Cars are often targeted by bailiffs because they are easy to seize and sell (at auction). Because of this, you may want to keep your vehicle parked well away from your property, or locked in a garage. Bailiffs may have the right to immobilise your vehicle with a wheel clamp, and may do so while waiting for a removal truck to take it away. If the bailiff seizes or impounds your vehicle, you will incur the additional costs of removal as well as the lower value of the auction sale. If a bailiff has clamped or is about to take possession of your vehicle, you should try to come to an arrangement with the bailiff as soon as possible.

A visit from the bailiff

With the exception of rent arrears, where goods must be seized between sunrise and sundown, a bailiff may call at any reasonable time, both at weekdays and at weekends. Bailiffs usually attempt to call at a time when they will stand the greatest chance of success, such as during business hours if you work from home, or at weekends, if you work Monday to Friday. A bailiff may call more than once.

Because bailiffs are aware that they must first gain access to your home before they can seize your goods, they may use some persuasive arguments to gain entry. You should remain on your guard to prevent this from happening. It has been known for bailiffs to push past people, climb through windows, break into cars and even trick you into letting them in by saying they want to make a phone call or use your toilet. Although it can seem unfair, the bailiff may have the backing of the court even if the method of entry has been unorthodox.

Arguments you may come across from bailiffs seeking to gain entry to your home include the following:

- **'I will call the police if I am refused access'** Bailiffs cannot use the police to gain access to your property; the only role the police play in these situations is to prevent a breach of the peace.
- **'I have the automatic right to seize your goods'** A bailiff must first gain access to your property in order to take walking possession of your goods, and can use force only when returning to seize your goods if previously let into your home. If you argue this point with the bailiff, he or she must back down.
- **'I have seen your goods through the window and taken a levy'** This argument does not stand up. It is, however, advisable to ensure that valuable goods are kept out of sight, because a description of your possessions will be given to the court and this may prejudice the likelihood that the court will be lenient.
- **'I have the right to take possession of your goods without gaining access'** Some bailiffs will put a note through your door claiming that all goods have been impounded and will be collected at a later date. It is, however, unlawful for a bailiff to take goods from you in this way, and the court will judge in your favour in the event of any such attempt.

If the bailiff gains access

When a bailiff has been into your property and taken a levy of goods, the law gives him or her the right to return to remove the goods, by force if necessary. Once inside, the bailiff has free access throughout your home, and may break down internal doors if he or she believes they have been locked because you have tried to stop the bailiff from gaining access to your possessions.

Bailiffs' fees

A bailiff's fee, paid by the creditor, is added to your debt. To dispute the amount successfully, you will need to demonstrate that the charges are unreasonable and do not reflect the actual costs incurred by the bailiffs. For more information on bailiffs' fees contact a debt adviser at your local CAB★ or National Debtline★.

How to make a complaint about a bailiff

If it seems clear to you that the bailiffs have acted unlawfully, rudely or aggressively, or have charged fees that are clearly unreasonable, it is well worth your time and effort making a complaint. Most bailiffs (and all council tax bailiffs) are certificated, which means that if the court agrees that they have acted unreasonably or illegally, they can be fined or have their licence revoked.

You can complain through your local county or magistrates' court, or the council pursuing the debt or your local councillor, if the council will not help you. You can also complain to the bailiff's professional or trade organisation. These bodies can impose penalties including fines and exclusion of membership. They may also reimburse your goods and/or fees. Find out from the court which body the bailiff belongs to and write to the Association of Civil Enforcement Agencies★ or the Certified Bailiffs Association★.

Bailiffs and the Human Rights Act

The new Human Rights Act, which came into force in October 2000, may see bailiffs being used less frequently. Part of the Act protects your right to 'peaceful enjoyment of possessions and respect for your privacy, family life and home'.

In practice, this will mean that courts and public authorities should use bailiffs only as a last resort, instead favouring less intrusive and distressing ways of getting you to pay the money you owe. These include:

- benefit deductions
- attachment of earnings (see pages 116–17), and
- voluntary payment arrangements.

National standards

In May 2002, following a review of court enforcement mechanisms, the government launched National Standards for Enforcement Agents in areas such as: professionalism and conduct of the enforcement agent, training and certification, complaints and discipline, and creditors' responsibilities.

The standards are intended for use by all enforcement agents, the enforcement agencies that employ them and the major creditors who use their services.

Copies of the National Standards for Enforcement Agents are available from the Lord Chancellor's Department (LCD) website*

Imprisonment

Being sent to prison is a major worry for many people with serious debts. In most cases, however, imprisonment is very unlikely, since a prison sentence is only a last resort. Also, imprisonment can result from only three types of debt:

- when you haven't paid court fines
- when you haven't paid your council tax

- when you haven't paid maintenance for your husband or wife or your children.

Imprisonment is likely to result only if the court believes that you won't pay, rather than can't pay, your debts. In other words, it considers that you have deliberately refused to pay, or that you have chosen to spend the money on inessential items. The court will generally only imprison people who refuse to make payments that it has ordered. You cannot be sent to prison without a hearing.

If you receive a warrant for your arrest, you should get legal advice and report to the police or magistrate's court. You have the right for a lawyer to speak for you even if you cannot afford to pay for one. The magistrate should give you time to speak to a duty solicitor at the court before your case is heard. This is important because, before any order is made committing you to prison, the court may write off all or part of your debt to make it easier for you to pay. Your solicitor may also be able to provide reasons that will prevent your imprisonment.

CHAPTER 9

Claiming benefits

A key priority in tackling debt is to maximise your income. For many people in financial difficulty this may mean claiming some form of Social Security benefit. It is important that you make sure you know what you are entitled to, as this could make all the difference. Note that the amounts given in this chapter may be liable to change. You can find the latest figures on the website of the Department for Work and Pensions (DWP).*

There are four main circumstances in which you can receive benefit:

- if you are on a low income
- if you are unemployed
- if you are sick or have a disability
- if you are bereaved.

People on a low income

Benefits for those on low incomes are of two kinds: Income Support and Tax Credits.

Income Support

Income Support is designed to help people aged between 16 and 59 who are on a low income, either because they are not working or they are working on average less than 16 hours a week. If you have savings of over £8,000 you usually won't be eligible for this benefit. If your savings are over £3,000 this will normally reduce the amount of Income Support you can get. If you have a partner who works an average of 24 hours a week or more you can't usually claim Income Support. If your partner works less than 24 hours a week, his or her earnings will affect the amount of Income Support you can get.

The amount you can claim depends on your individual circumstances. Income Support is made up of a weekly personal allowance, which depends on your age and whether you are single, part of a couple or have dependent children. Extra premiums are paid if you are a pensioner, have a severe disability or you are a carer. In addition, you may be awarded a further premium to cover housing costs – again this will depend on your individual circumstances.

How to claim

Contact your Social Security office for a claim form. You can find your local office on the DWP website* or look for the Benefits Agency display advert in the phone book.

Tax Credits

From April 2003, Children's Tax Credit, Working Families' Tax Credit and Disabled Person's Tax Credit are replaced by two new credits: Child Tax Credit and Working Tax Credit. The new tax credits also replace any money received for children through Income Support, Income-Based Jobseeker's Allowance and the New Deal 50+ Employment Credit.

If you have children, you are likely to get some tax credit if your income (joint income if you are a couple) is less than £58,000 a year, or £66,000 if you have a child under the age of one. If you don't have children you are likely to get some tax credit if your income (joint income for couples) is less than £13,500 a year. Couples may qualify whether or not they are married. Same-sex couples should make individual claims.

What counts as income?

For the purpose of calculating whether you are eligible for Tax Credits your 'income' means:

- your gross taxable income from employment and/or self-employment after the deduction of pension contributions and Gift Aid payments
- income from state or private pensions
- interest on savings in a bank or building society (but not individual savings accounts (ISAs) or other tax-free savings accounts)
- income from any property you let (but not income from letting a furnished room in your home if the income is less than £4,250)
- income from a trust
- foreign income.

However, any income of £300 a year or less from pensions, savings, property and foreign income is ignored, as are maintenance payments for children and Child Benefit, among other things.

The amount of Tax Credit you will be awarded for the 2003–4 tax year is based on the income you received in 2001–2. If your income is likely to be less for the year 6 April 2003 to 5 April 2004, you should notify your tax office as soon as you receive your award. You may be entitled to extra credit. Equally if you expect your income for the year to 5 April 2004 to be more than £2,500 above your income for

the year to 5 April 2002 you must tell your tax office immediately. If you don't, you may have to pay back any overpayment after 5 April 2004. If you are not eligible for an
award because your income in 2001–2 was too high, but you
are eligible now, contact your Tax Office.

Child Tax Credit

Child Tax Credit is a payment for families with children. You
can claim for a dependent child up to 16 years old, or for a
young person aged 16 to 18 who:

- is in full-time education, up to and including 'A' levels,
  NVQ level 3 or Scottish Highers
- has left full-time education but does not have a job or
  training place and has registered with the Careers Service
  or Connexions Service
- is not claiming Income Support or Tax Credits in his or
  her own right
- is not serving a custodial sentence of four months or more.

You can claim if you are single (or separated), a married
couple or a man and woman living together as if you are
married. You don't have to be working to claim Child Tax
Credit, but if you are you may get a higher amount. Child
Tax Credit will be paid directly to the person who is mainly
responsible for caring for the children in the family.

How much can you claim?

The amount of Child Tax Credit you receive increases for each
child (or young person) you are responsible for. You will also
receive a higher rate, known as the 'baby element', if one or
more children in the family is under one year old (you don't
get extra for each child). The Tax Credit is increased further if
you are responsible for a child or children with a disability. You

will receive a higher rate for each child if you are receiving Disability Living Allowance for the child or the child is registered blind or has been taken off the blind register in the 28 weeks before the date of the claim. A higher payment known as the 'severe disability element' is paid if you receive Disability Living Allowance (Highest Care Component) for the child. You also get more if you are working more than 16 hours a week if you are a lone parent, or you are both working more than 16 hours a week if you are part of a couple.

Working Tax Credit

Working Tax Credit is a payment to top up the earnings of working people on low incomes. There are extra amounts for people with a disability, people who have to pay for childcare or are over 50. Working Tax Credit is for people who are employed or self-employed, either on their own or in partnership, and who are:

- aged 16 or over and responsible for at least one child, or
- aged 16 or over and have a disability, or
- aged 25 or over and usually work at least 30 hours a week, or
- aged 50 or over and have recently started work after qualifying for certain benefits for at least six months.

Working Tax Credit is paid in addition to any Child Tax Credit you may be entitled to.

How much can you claim?

Working tax credit is made up of different elements – you will receive one or more of these elements depending on your circumstances.

- **Basic element** – paid to any working person who meets the conditions

- **Lone parent element** – for lone parents
- **Couples element** – for couples
- **30-hour element** – for people who work at least 30 hours a week. Couples with at least one child can claim the 30-hour element if they work at least 30 hours a week between them
- **Disability element** – for working people with disabilities
- **Severe disability element** – for people claiming Disability Living Allowance (Highest Care Component) or Attendance Allowance (Higher Rate)
- **50-plus element** – for people aged 50 or over who have just returned to work after a period on benefit
- **Childcare element** – for working families who spend money on approved childcare. In 2003 you can claim up to a maximum of £94.50 a week for one child or £140 a week for two or more children. To claim, lone parents must work 16 hours a week or more, couples must both work 16 hours a week or more, unless one parent is prevented from working by incapacity.

Getting your entitlement

You can find out how much Child Tax Credit and Working Tax Credit you are entitled to and register online by going to the Inland Revenue website* Alternatively, you can check whether you are eligible and/or get a claim pack by telephoning the Inland Revenue Tax Credits Information Line (0800) 500222 (see *IRWTC1 Child Tax Credit and Working Tax Credit – An Introduction*). One form covers both Tax Credits.

The new Tax Credit system is complicated, but don't let that put you off. Thousands of people – and an estimated nine out of ten families – are entitled to receive these new tax credits.

Council Tax Benefit

You may be able to get a deduction on the council tax you pay if you are on a low income. The amount varies depending on your income.

If you have savings over £16,000 you will usually not be eligible to claim Council Tax Benefit. Savings of between £3,000 (£6,000 if you or your partner are aged over 60) and £16,000 will affect how much council tax benefit you can get.

Unemployed people

Jobseeker's Allowance (JSA) was introduced in October 1996 and replaced Unemployment Benefit and Income Support for the unemployed. There are two types of Jobseeker's Allowance – contribution-based and income-based.

Contribution-based Jobseeker's Allowance

You will receive a contribution-based allowance if you have made a sufficient level of National Insurance payments. Your Jobcentre Plus or Jobcentre can tell you how much this is. You can't claim contribution-based JSA if you have only been paying National Insurance contributions for self-employment, although you may be entitled to Income-Based JSA (see below).

Contribution-Based JSA is paid at a fixed rate depending on your age, for up to 26 weeks. The amount you receive might be reduced if you have an occupational or personal pension over a certain amount.

If you are entitled to contribution-based JSA but your income is still below the legal minimum, you may also be able to get some Income-Based JSA, which is means-tested.

Income-Based Jobseeker's Allowance

If you have savings of over £8,000 you usually can't get Income-Based JSA. If you or your partner are aged 60 or over, this savings limit goes up to £12,000. Any savings over £3,000 (or £6,000 if you or your partner are aged 60 or over) usually affect how much Income-Based JSA you can get. Any occupational or personal pension income you receive will also be taken into account.

If you have a partner or spouse who works an average of 24 hours a week or more, you will not usually be entitled to Income-Based JSA. This does not affect your right to Contribution-Based JSA. If you have a partner who works an average of less than 24 hours a week, his or her earnings will usually affect the amount of Income-Based JSA you can get.

Qualifying for Jobseeker's Allowance

To be eligible to receive Jobseeker's Allowance you must:

- be a UK citizen
- be working less than 16 hours of paid employment a week, or be out of work while you are claiming
- not usually be a student in full-time study although you may be eligible in some circumstances.
- be under the earnings threshold and have savings below the maximum level set by the government
- not have left your previous job voluntarily or because of misconduct.

Jobseeker Interviews

To claim JSA you must attend a New Jobseeker Interview (at your Jobcentre Plus or JobCentre). You will have to complete a claim form beforehand which you will need to bring with you. At the interview, an adviser will:

- make sure you understand the rules for JSA
- discuss the kinds of work you are looking for and the best ways of finding a job
- give you information about jobs, training and other opportunities
- check that you have filled in your form correctly and given all the information required.

Jobseeker's Agreement

To get JSA you must have a Jobseeker's Agreement. You will make this agreement with an advisor at the Jobseeker interview, and you will both sign it. Your Jobseeker's Agreement will include details of:

- your availability for work
- the kind of work you are looking for
- what you will do to look for work and improve your chances of finding work
- how Jobcentre Plus can help you.

After you have made a successful claim

You must usually attend the Jobcentre every two weeks to confirm that you are still entitled to JSA. Your Jobcentre adviser will discuss how your job search is going and how he or she may be able to help you. In addition, you must also go to regular, more detailed interviews to review your suitability for work.

If you take voluntary early retirement you may not get JSA straight away. If you are a man aged between 60 and 64, you can choose instead to get Minimum Income Guarantee through your Jobcentre and/or claim Income Support.

If you are sick

You are entitled to take at least two periods off sick in each 12-month period while you are signed on. During this period, which can be for a maximum of two weeks, you will not be expected to be actively seeking work, and will not have to provide evidence of your job search at the fortnightly interview. If your sickness period goes on for more than two weeks you will need to make a fresh claim, and you may consider claiming incapacity benefit instead.

If you are working part-time or earning money

The rules for claiming JSA if you are earning money are straightforward. Once you earn over a certain amount, deductions are made from each fortnightly payment that you receive.

Earnings include:

- wages, salary and any expenses paid by an employer not exclusively connected with carrying out your job
- bonuses or commission
- most holiday pay
- certain payments made under the Employment Rights Act 1996 and the Trade Union and Labour Relations (Consolidation) Acts 1992.

Earnings do not include:

- regular payments made as part of a redundancy package
- payments made in respect of a period of maternity leave or absence from work because of illness
- payments wholly connected with your employment such as travelling expenses, clothing or telephone costs.

Reasons for withdrawal of JSA

If you fail to follow the minimum requirements for claiming Jobseeker's Allowance, your claim can be denied and you will lose your right to receive payments. The following are reasons why your claim might be stopped or action taken against you:

- you fail to actively seek work
- you earn more than the maximum limit for eligibility
- you fail to attend your fortnightly review meeting without giving a good reason for doing so
- you failed to attend a review meeting designed to test the validity of your claim
- you refuse to complete a mandatory programme such as Jobplan
- you refuse or fail to take employment that has been offered to you without providing an adequate reason for doing so.

The most common outcome of failing to meet the requirements of the Jobseeker's programme is that your benefit will be stopped for a minimum of two weeks. This may be increased to a minimum of four weeks if it is the second time that you have failed to meet the requirements. You should speak to the Benefits Agency as soon as possible if there is a good reason for your inability to meet the requirements – for example, illness.

Hardship provision

You will not usually be able to get JSA until you have a Jobseeker's Agreement. In some situations you may be able to get a reduced allowance under the hardship provision, even if your JSA cannot be paid under normal rules. You must be able to show that you or someone in your household will suffer hardship if you do not receive any JSA. This might be the case if you or your partner:

- are looking after children
- are single and looking after a 16-or 17-year-old

- have a disability
- are pregnant
- have a long-term physical medical condition
- are caring for someone who is long-term sick or has a disability
- are a young person who has left local authority care in the last three years
- are aged 16 or 17, in some circumstances.

People who are sick or have a disability

If you are unable to work because of sickness or a disability you may be entitled to benefits.

Statutory Sick Pay (SSP)

You can receive this if you are employed. The right to receive SSP is dependent on the employee having worked for the employer for three months continuously and having made adequate National Insurance contributions. It is payable for up to 28 weeks in any three-year period. If you have more than one job you may be entitled to SSP from each employer. If you are still unable to work when SSP ends, you should claim Incapacity Benefit (see below). If you meet the lower earnings limit for National Insurance contributions (£77 per week in 2003–4) the standard rate payable is £64.35 a week, subject to the deduction of tax and National Insurance contributions.

Incapacity Benefit

Incapacity Benefit is payable when SSP has ended or you aren't eligible to receive SSP. It is also payable if you are pregnant and can't get Statutory Maternity Pay or Maternity Allowance (MA) and you have paid National Insurance contributions.

It is not paid if you were over state pension age when you became sick. You can claim Incapacity Benefit if you have paid adequate National Insurance contributions and have been incapable of work because of sickness or disability for at least four days in a row, including weekends and public holidays.

Incapacity Benefit can be paid at three different rates depending on your age and the length of your illness. The rules for benefits mean your individual circumstances may alter the amount you can get.

Claiming Incapacity Benefit

Contact your Social Security Office for a claim form. Find your local office by checking out the DWP website★, or look for 'Jobcentre Plus' or 'Social Security' in the phone book. Alternatively, you can ring the Benefit Enquiry Line (BEL)★. The BEL is a confidential telephone service available for people with disabilities, their representatives and their carers. People with speech or hearing problems can use the BEL textphone★ for general advice. You can also get leaflets and claim forms from the BEL.

Disability Living Allowance (DLA)

This benefit is paid to people who have a disability and need help getting around, or need help looking after themselves. You must normally claim DLA before you reach the age of 65. Different rates are paid depending on how your disability affects you. You can also claim DLA for a child with a severe physical or mental illness or disability.

Attendance Allowance

This benefit is paid if you become ill or develop a disability on or after your 65th birthday and you need help looking after yourself. There are two rates depending on whether you need care during the day, night or both. You can claim if you have savings, and other income does not usually affect eligibility.

Bereavement benefits

There are three types of benefit that may be payable if your husband or wife dies (see below). To claim these you must have been legally married – you are not eligible if you were divorced from or cohabiting with your late partner – and your late husband or wife must have either paid adequate National Insurance contributions (your own don't count), or his or her death must have been caused by his or her job. You may continue to receive Widowed Mother's Allowance or Widow's Pension, which were replaced by the current benefits in 2001, provided you meet the relevant criteria.

Bereavement Payment

This is a tax-free payment of £2,000 paid to you as soon as your spouse dies. It is payable only if your late husband or wife was not entitled to the state retirement pension when he or she died or you were under state pension age. Those in receipt of state pension are not entitled to this payment.

Widowed Parent's Allowance

This is a taxable weekly benefit. It includes:

- a basic allowance for you
- an allowance for each of your dependent children, and
- additional pension (state earnings-related pension) if you qualify.

You are eligible for Widowed Parent's Allowance if you have a child who qualifies for Child Benefit or you are a woman expecting your late husband's baby. If you are a widower whose wife died before the introduction of Widowed Parent's Allowance in 2001, you can still claim provided you meet the entitlement conditions.

Bereavement Allowance

This is a taxable weekly benefit paid for 52 weeks after your husband or wife dies, to people aged 45 or over. You won't get bereavement allowance if you are entitled to Widowed Parent's Allowance.

Housing Benefit

Housing Benefit is paid by local councils to people living on benefits or low incomes to help them with their rent. If you are a private or housing association tenant it is some-times called 'rent allowance'. If you are a council tenant it is sometimes called a 'rent rebate'. This assistance is not available for householders to help pay mortgage interest. If you receive Income Support or Income-Based Jobseeker's Allowance you may be able to get help with this as part of your benefit.

Am I eligible to claim?

Housing Benefit is offered to people out of work and claiming state benefit, as well as those on low incomes who are working either full- or part-time. It is worth making a claim if you believe that you might be eligible. Housing Benefit can help to ease the burden on your budget and safeguard your home against repossession. You cannot claim if you are living with your parents or close relatives, or you are a full-time student.

How do I claim Housing Benefit?

To claim Housing Benefit you will first need to apply to the local council's Housing Benefit department. You will be required to provide proof to validate your claim, including details of your address, the address of your landlord, your tenancy agreement, rent, income and family members who live with you. Other information may also be required, such as your National Insurance number, passport or birth certificate.

The council will normally take at least two weeks to process your claim, so you should ensure that you apply as soon as you become eligible. Your claim will be backdated to when the council first received your completed claim form. You can hand your application in immediately, even if some of the information you provide is incomplete (you will have to supply full details later). If you think that you will have difficulty in completing a claim form, you should speak to your Housing Benefit department. If you have a good reason for having not applied earlier, for example you were unwell, you should bring this to the council's attention. If there is a delay in assessing your application you may be entitled to an interim payment of Housing Benefit (see page 153).

How is Housing Benefit calculated?

Although the amount of Housing Benefit you receive will be based on your income, or lack of it, the calculations involved can be quite complex and take a number of other factors into account:

- **your income** If your income is higher than what you would get on Income Support or Jobseeker's Allowance, the Housing Benefit you are entitled to will be reduced accordingly. The more you earn, the less you'll receive.

- **your savings or capital** The amount of Housing Benefit you are entitled to receive will begin to be affected if you have savings of £3,000 or more. If you have over £16,000 in savings you will not be eligible to receive any Housing Benefit at all.

- **your rent** Most applications for Housing Benefit are assessed by the council's rent officer to ensure that the rent is not too expensive compared to similar properties in the area and that your home is not too large for your household, based on how many rooms you occupy and the number of people living in them. If this is the case, Housing Benefit will be reduced by means of a 'rent restriction'. If your tenancy started before 15 January 1989, or you are a council tenant, these restrictions will not apply.

- **your dependants** You may be entitled to receive additional Housing Benefit if you have dependants living with you for whom you are responsible. Conversely, benefit may be reduced if you have people living with you who are over 18 and not responsible for paying part of the rent, if they could be expected to make a contribution

- **your age** If you are single and under 25 years old, the benefit you receive will be based on single-room accommodation at the local market value.

- **other factors** Some rent payments include components such as water, electricity bills and service charges. Housing Benefit is not designed to cover these extras, only the principal cost of the rent itself.

What should I do if my circumstances change?

If you are receiving Housing Benefit and your circumstances change, you are required to contact the Housing Benefit department so that your claim can be adjusted. You will be expected to declare changes in income, any change regarding the people living with you and changes of address. If you receive a windfall that increases your savings over the £3,000 limit at which the amount of Housing Benefit you get is affected, this also needs to be declared.

Can I check my Housing Benefit entitlement before I move in?

It is possible to get a good idea of how much Housing Benefit you are entitled to before you move in. You must first decide on a property in which you intend to live, and ask the Benefits Agency to carry out a free pre-tenancy determination (PTD). The Benefits Agency will tell you if it will pay any Housing Benefit on that property. You can apply for more than one PTD. A PTD form can be obtained from the council's Housing Benefit department. The landlord will need to sign the form to give the rent officer the right to attend the property. The rent officer must respond within five days of your application.

How is Housing Benefit paid?

Housing Benefit is normally paid directly to you, although you can ask for it to be paid directly to your landlord. If you are a council tenant it will be paid directly into your rent account. If you are more than eight weeks in arrears with your rent, the council may order the payments to be made directly to your landlord.

Payments of Housing Benefit are generally made at monthly intervals. If you decide you want your Housing Benefit claim to be backdated, you will only be able to request this with good reason (such as illness). The maximum period that the council can backdate the payment is 52 weeks from the date that your request is made. You will be advised to seek help if you want to apply for your claim to be backdated.

The council should make a payment to you within 14 days of receiving your claim form. If it fails to do this, you will be entitled to an interim payment, which is an estimate of the amount that the council thinks that it owes you. If you are about to be evicted, you will be able to apply for an urgent payment to avoid eviction from the Housing Benefit department or the Housing Advice Service. If the Benefits Agency subsequently decides that this payment is too high, it can take action against you to recover the overpayment.

Can I appeal against a Housing Benefit decision?

If you are denied Housing Benefit or you feel that the amount that you have been awarded is not sufficient, you have the right to appeal. The first step in making the appeal is to ask for a written explanation of the amount granted, called a 'statement of reasons'. If you are not satisfied with this, you must write to the council within six weeks explaining why you disagree. If you are not satisfied with the council's subsequent response, you can request a further review by the Housing Benefit Review Board. A hearing will be arranged and you will be expected to attend, although you may request that a solicitor, friend or financial adviser be present to represent you. It is strongly advised that you do this. At the hearing, the panel of local councillors will decide whether or not to alter the award. You will be notified of their decision in due course.

Avoiding homelessness

If you are in serious debt and on a low income, the threat of homelessness can be one of the biggest fears that you have to face. It is vital that you become aware of all the steps you can take to prevent the prospect of becoming homeless.

Emergency housing

The local council has an obligation to provide emergency accommodation for certain people who have nowhere to live. Under Part 7 of the Housing Act 1996 the council will have to provide you with accommodation if you:

- are actually, or about to be, made homeless
- are eligible for assistance
- are in priority need
- have not made yourself 'intentionally homeless'
- have a local connection.

If you meet the criteria, the local council must find you accommodation, including emergency accommodation if you are homeless, the same day.

What counts as homelessness?

The council will consider you to be homeless if you are actually homeless, or you are facing homelessness within 28 days. It might also consider you to be homeless if you are living in accommodation that is either unfit for habitation, not suitable for your particular medical needs or you are experiencing or being threatened by violence.

Eligible for assistance

A person who is not eligible for assistance is owed no duty under homelessness law. In addition, an ineligible person cannot be taken into account when deciding whether someone else is homeless or in priority need.

A person will not be considered 'eligible' if he or she is somebody who needs permission to enter the UK and who does not have recourse to public funds or is not habitually resident in the UK. This situation will cover most asylum seekers. It may also apply to people who are from a member country within the European Union (EU) or are UK citizens who are coming to the UK after a long period of absence.

As making a homelessness application might affect your rights to remain in the UK, if you are in any doubt as to whether or not you or a member of your household is eligible, seek advice before approaching the council for housing assistance.

Priority-need cases

The council has a duty of care to help people to find housing if they have special needs. You will be considered to be in priority need if you or somebody living in your household:

- are vulnerable a) because of sickness or old age; b) because you have been looked after, accommodated or fostered by the local authority and are over 21; c) you have been in the

Armed Forces; d) you have been in prison; e) you have ceased to occupy accommodation as a result of violence or threats of violence.

- are pregnant or living with someone who is pregnant
- have dependent children living with you
- have become homeless because of a flood, fire or other disaster
- are 16 or 17 years old
- are between 18 and 21 years of age and have been looked after or accommodated by Social Services.

Intentional homelessness

You may find it difficult to get housed if the council believes that you have knowingly, or deliberately, contrived to make yourself homeless. It may take this view if:

- you have been found somewhere suitable to stay but you have turned it down without an adequate reason
- you have chosen to leave your current address without an adequate reason
- you told your landlord to tell you to leave
- you became homeless because of the behaviour and/or actions of somebody else and you did not take steps to prevent this.

You might not be considered intentionally homeless if:

- you had to leave your address because you did not have enough money to continue to live there
- you are living under the threat of violence
- the property in which you are living is not suitable for habitation, unless you contrived to make it that way
- the property in which you are living is not suitable for your particular medical needs

- someone else contrived to make you homeless, and you had no control over his or her actions
- you left the property in good faith, believing that you did not have the right to stay there.

Proving a local connection

Before the council will consider housing you, you will need to show that you have a local connection with the area in which you are applying. To qualify, you or a member of your household must meet one of the following conditions:

- you must have lived in the area for at least six months out of the last 12 or at least three years out of the last five years
- you work in the area
- you have a close family connection in the area and he or she has lived in the area for at least five years
- you need to be in the area for some other special reason, for example, you are receiving support from people in the area which would not be available elsewhere.

If you do not have a local connection then you will be referred to a council in an area where you do satisfy the above requirements, unless it is not safe for you to return to that area due to violence. If you have just entered the UK, the council that you approach first must deal with your request.

Successful applicants

If you meet the above requirements, the local council will be under an obligation to find you temporary accommodation immediately. It is important that you don't turn this down, unless you have a very good reason for doing so, because you may not be offered anywhere else. If you feel that you do have a very good reason for refusing the accommodation

that is offered to you, you should always seek advice before
turning it down.

While you are in temporary accommodation the council
will expect you to co-operate with it in finding permanent
accommodation from the council's waiting list or from
another source. The council may withdraw its help if you:

- become ineligible for help from the council
- become intentionally homeless from accommodation
  made available for your occupation
- unreasonably refuse alternative accommodation from the
  council's waiting list
- find somewhere else to live.

Applying for housing

You should apply through the Homeless Persons Unit of
your local council. If you are about to be made homeless and
your situation is urgent, it is important that you make this
clear to the officer who is dealing with your claim. If possible
take some evidence with you to support your claim, such as
an eviction notice and a statement of your means, in order to
demonstrate that you are unable to afford to pay for somewhere else to live. You may also be asked to provide proof of
your identity.

The council waiting list

When you apply for housing you will need to put your
name down on the council's waiting list for permanent
accommodation. The length of time that you will have to
wait for this accommodation will depend on how urgent the
council considers your situation is, and whether you are a
priority need case (see pages 155–6).

Appealing against the council's decision

If the council either refuses to accept your homelessness application or to provide you with emergency accommodation, you may have to consider taking legal action in court. If, following its enquiries, the council decides that for any reason it does not need to provide you with accommodation, you also have the right to request a review of its decision. You will have 21 days from the date of the letter notifying you of the decision to request a review.

In either situation, you are advised to contact an advice agency, such as Shelter★ or the Citizens Advice Bureau (CAB)★, which will examine your claim and help you to challenge the council if it appears that it has acted incorrectly.

Where to find help

For more advice, see the Community Legal Service's leaflet *Losing Your Home* available at Citizens Advice Bureaux and online at www.justask.

If you need to be rehoused or have concerns about accommodation-related issues you can obtain help and advice from the following organisations:

- Shelterline – a 24-hour, free, national housing helpline run by the charity Shelter★
- your local housing aid centre – contact Shelter for details
- your local Citizens Advice Bureau★
- a local law centre specialising in housing issues.

Emergency borrowing

Crisis Loans

If you are in serious debt or on a low income it is likely that from time to time you will run out of money completely and have no means of sustaining yourself over the days or weeks before you receive your next payment. The government has money set aside in a Social Fund to help people in serious financial difficulty, regardless of whether or not they are currently claiming benefit. These payments are made in the form of a Crisis Loan, available from the DWP*.

Crisis Loans are particularly suitable for people who are not receiving other state benefits.

Why you might need a Crisis Loan

The most common reasons for seeking a Crisis Loan are:

- you have just found a job and will not be receiving your first payment for some time. (Payments for daily living expenses can often be provided for the full period until you receive your first payment)
- you are currently, or about to be, made homeless, and not getting the loan would cause you to spend time sleeping rough
- you need funds while cashing in assets that are large enough to have precluded you from being able to claim state benefits
- you are experiencing an enforced break in your employment without pay
- you do not have enough money to pay for travel expenses to get you back home
- you need the money to prevent essential fuel supplies from being disconnected
- you need the money to pay for the aftermath of a disaster such as fire or flood.

Qualifying for a Crisis Loan

Although there is no automatic right to a Crisis Loan and eligibility depends on your personal circumstances, so long as you meet *all* the criteria listed below, it is likely that you will qualify.

1) You must be able to prove that you are suffering from severe financial hardship and you need the money to prevent serious health problems from causing distress to you or your family. Not having enough money to afford food or shelter are usually good enough reasons.
2) You have a private landlord and you will be evicted unless your rent arrears are paid immediately.
3) You are over 16 years old.
4) You are able to repay the loan (deductions from future benefit are usually an acceptable method of achieving this).
5) You are eligible (full-time students, people in hospital or care, people in custody or people subject to Jobseeker's Allowance, disallowances or sanctions are excluded in most cases).
6) The loan is not for an excluded item, such as telephone services, running or maintenance of a car, holidays or television and radio.

Amount of the award

The amount you are likely to receive depends on your personal circumstances. If you have savings of more than £500 (£1,000 if you or your partner are over 60) the amount you get will be reduced. If you have already borrowed from the Social Fund and have not yet paid back your loan, this will also affect the amount you can get. The maximum amount awarded for a crisis loan is £1,000. Any amount awarded will be discretionary and depends on your personal circumstances. You will not have to provide evidence of the price of the item that you are claiming for, but if the price seems to be too great it will probably be queried. If you need the money to repair or replace an essential utility such as a cooker, the loan will go towards paying for the least expensive option.

If you need money just to help you to get by, the amount normally paid is up to 75 per cent of the usual Jobseeker's Allowance payment for you or your partner, and £31.45 per week for each child.

Applying for a Crisis Loan

Time is usually of the essence when you need a Crisis Loan, so the money will normally be made available to you on the same day that you apply. The payment will be made in cash or by giro cheque that can be cashed at a post office on the day of issue. Alternatively, payment may be made in the form of cash or vouchers, or paid directly to your landlord or to the supplier of the product that you need to purchase or have repaired.

Your application for a Crisis Loan is made on form SF401, and a second form SF400 is completed at the interview.

Repaying the loan

Repayments are made directly to the DWP. There is no minimum period for repaying the Crisis Loan, but the DWP will usually expect repayment to be made in full within 78 weeks.

If you are working, deductions can be made by increasing the amount of tax that you pay, by making changes to your tax code. If you are on a tight budget, you can negotiate with the DWP regarding the amount of the deduction.

Because a Crisis Loan is interest-free, and repayments are likely to be very low, paying back the loan may not present you with a high degree of hardship, especially if you are receiving an outside income. However, if it is causing you financial hardship, you should tell the Benefits Officer so that you can come to an alternative arrangement.

Budgeting Loans

If you have been claiming Income Support or Income-Based Jobseeker's Allowance for more than 26 weeks, you may be entitled to a loan from the DWP to provide funding for inter-mittent expenses that crop up from time to time. Although they have to be repaid, Budgeting Loans are easier to obtain than CCGs, provided you meet the eligibility requirements.

Budgeting Loans cover:

- furniture and household equipment
- clothing and footwear
- rent in advance and/or removal expenses to secure fresh accommodation
- home improvement, maintenance and security
- travelling expenses
- expenses associated with seeking or re-entering work
- hire purchase and other debts for any of the above items.

Loans of £30 to £1,000 may be awarded. The amount that you will get will depend on what the loan is for, how much you will be able to afford to repay, and how long you have been receiving benefit.

CHAPTER 10

Credit and borrowing

A consequence of failing to deal with debt, defaulting on repayments or incurring legal action from creditors is that your 'credit rating' will suffer. This is because potential lenders will view you as a bad risk. Some companies are prepared to extend credit to borrowers that others would turn down, but charge a high rate of interest for taking this risk (see non-standard lenders, page 177).

Credit scoring

The most common method used to assess applications for credit is a statistical technique called 'credit scoring'. This has the advantage of being objective and – because it is easily computerised – quick (which is why it is possible to apply for a loan over the phone).

Each of the answers you give when you apply for credit is given a score. If your application scores more than the lender's pass-mark, you will get the credit; if it scores less than the pass-mark, you will not (although borderline cases may be assessed individually). Because credit scoring is based on the statistical analysis of a lender's past experiences, different lenders use different scoring systems and pass-marks. The scoring systems generally reflect common sense: if you are tied to your home by your mortgage, have a steady job and a good history of repaying your debts, for example, you will probably score more highly than if you live in a rented flat, have a temporary job and have never had credit before. Credit scoring is not used simply to accept or reject your application: it may also be used to decide the rate of interest you pay and/or how much you can borrow. Your credit score will also be affected by the information the lender gets from a credit reference agency.

Credit reference agencies

Lenders use credit reference agencies to discover information on how much credit you have applied for and on how good you are at making repayments. Contrary to popular opinion, these agencies do not keep blacklists nor do they give an opinion on your creditworthiness – it is up to the lender to decide whether the details supplied make you a good or bad credit risk. The main credit reference agencies are Callcredit*, Experian* and Equifax* and the kind of information they keep about you includes:

- your entry on the electoral roll
- records of County Court Judgments (CCJs) (decrees in Scotland) for non-payment of debt
- details of any bankruptcies
- details of your other loans and credit cards – both current and those you have had in the past
- how often you have applied for credit
- how well you have kept up your repayments and whether you have defaulted on any credit agreements in the past
- records about other people who live at the same address as you and/or who are financially connected to you.

What to do if you are turned down for credit

You could be turned down for credit for one of three reasons: you are under 18; you are not the kind of customer the lender is looking for; or you are not considered to be a good credit risk. If you are refused credit because of your age or customer 'profile', you cannot do very much about it. However, if on applying for a current account, a credit card or any other sort of loan you are turned down because you are considered to be a bad risk, you *can* do something about it by discovering the reasons for the refusal (see below). You should remember, though, that no one has an automatic right to credit, and if the lender has turned you down because it seems unlikely that you will be able to repay the loan, this suggests that you are asking for too much credit.

Appealing against a rejection

Although it is unlikely that the lender will give precise details of why it refused your application, you should be told whether your credit score let you down or you were rejected as a result of information supplied by a credit reference agency.

Provided you write to the lender within 28 days you are legally entitled to ask whether a credit reference agency was used, and if so which one (see Example letter, overleaf). The lender *must* give you this information (although it does not have to tell you what the agency said about you). You should get a reply within seven days of the lender receiving your letter.

Example of a letter appealing against a rejection

[Your address]

[Lending company's name]
[Address]
[Date]

Dear Ms Lender

Your reference: 5559asl

Following your letter of [date] rejecting my application for a personal loan of [amount], I am writing to ask why my application has been turned down.

If a credit reference agency was used in considering my application, please send me the name and address of the agency you used in accordance with my rights under section 157 of the Consumer Credit Act 1974.

I expect a reply within seven working days of your receiving this letter.

Yours sincerely

Name

How to get hold of your credit file

If your application for credit has been turned down and you ask the lender the name of the credit reference agency it used (see Example, above), you should get a reply from the lender naming the agency within seven days of it receiving your letter. To get hold of a copy of your credit file, you then need to write to the credit reference agency enclosing a cheque or postal order for £2 (see Example, below). You can also pay the fee by debit or credit card if you apply for a copy of your file online. However you apply, you need to provide:

- your full name and address including post code
- the length of time that you have lived at your current address
- details of any other addresses at which you have lived in the past six years
- if you are self-employed as a sole trader, the same details as above for your business.

Example of letter asking for a copy of your credit file

[Your address]

[Callcredit/Equifax/Experian]
[Address]
[Date]

Dear Callcredit/Equifax/Experian

In accordance with my rights under section 158(1) of the Consumer Credit Act 1974, I am writing to request a copy of my file and I enclose a cheque for £2.

My full name is [name] and I have lived at the address above since [date]. Before that date, my address was [address].

Please reply to this letter within seven days of receiving it.

Yours faithfully

Name

What to do when you get the file

Unless the agency replies asking you for more details to help trace your file, you should receive a copy of your file seven working days after your letter reached the agency. The copy of your file will be divided into different sections covering:

- **electoral roll information** which details your address and how long you have lived there. The names of previous occupants of the property will also be shown.

- **a record of inquiries** about your file which the agency has received in the last one to two years (depending on the agency), showing the type of inquiry and who made it

- **court information** which shows whether you have any CCJs or administration orders against you for non-payment of debt. Debts you were ordered to pay by a court which you paid within one month should not appear; debts repaid after one month may be marked 'satisfied' but stay on your file for six years

- **public record information** from sources other than court records – such as official gazettes and the Insolvency Service★ – may also appear

- **insight account information** which is the information provided by lenders on a monthly basis. This is where you will find your current credit details and whether your repayments are up to date. This may be shown as a series of codes in reverse date order: 0 means you paid on time; 1 that a payment is one month late; 2 that it is two months late and so on. 'S' means that you have settled the loan. Some lenders supply only default information, so if you have an immaculate record of paying your debts, this section may be blank

- **Credit Industry Fraud Avoidance System infor-mation** which could appear if a fraudster has attempted to use your name and address to get credit.

What to do if the file is wrong

As well as a copy of the file itself, you should receive a statement which sets out your rights under the Consumer Credit Act 1974 and the Data Protection Act 1998. This sets out what you are legally entitled to do if there is a wrong entry on your file. You can correct your file because it is factually incorrect or because the file is factually correct but could create a misleading impression without further explanation.

Correcting your file

If you think that an entry on your file is wrong and you believe that you will suffer as a result of the mistake, you are legally entitled to get the file corrected. Write to the agency explaining why you think that the entry is wrong and what you want the agency to do about it (see Example, overleaf). If you have documents which will support your case, it may help to streamline the correction process if you enclose copies of these. The agency should reply to your letter within 28 days of receiving it. The reply should tell you whether the entry has been corrected (in which case you will receive a copy of the correction) or removed, or whether the agency has taken no action.

Example of letter asking for a file to be corrected

[Your address]

[Callcredit/Equifax/Experian]
[Address]
[Date]

Dear Callcredit/Equifax/Experian

File reference: 987654321/1234

I am writing to ask you to make two corrections to my file in accordance with my rights under section 159 of the Consumer Credit Act 1974.

1. The County Court Judgment of [date] for non-payment of a debt of [amount] was not against me but against my cousin [name], who was living with me at the time but who now lives in [city/country]. Please remove this item from my file.

2. The file states that I am three months behind with my ABC personal loan repayments, which is not the case. I enclose a copy of the letter from ABC Finance Company confirming that all my repayments have been paid on time. Please amend the information on my file to reflect this fact.

I look forward to hearing from you within 28 days from the date you receive this letter.

Yours sincerely

Name

Adding a note of correction

If you are not happy with the correction, or the agency tells you that it has made no changes to your file or it does not reply within 28 days of receiving your letter, you have the right to compose your own 'note of correction'. This should be no longer than 200 words long and it should give a clear and accurate explanation of why you think the entry is incorrect. You can also write a note of correction if an entry on your file is factually correct but could be misleading without further explanation (see Example, below). If you need to do this, you should write to the agency within 28 days of its reply to your first letter (or the deadline for its reply if you did not get one). Your letter should tell the agency to add your note of correction to your file and to include a copy of it whenever information included on the uncorrected entry is given out.

Once the agency has received your note of correction, it has 28 days in which to let you know whether or not it will accept it and add it to your file.

Example of a letter sending a note of correction

[Your address]

[Callcredit/Equifax/Experian]
[Address]
[Date]

Dear Callcredit/Equifax/Experian

File reference: 987633331/1897

Thank you for your letter dated [date] telling me that you do not propose to make the correction I asked for in my letter dated [date].

Please add the following note of correction to my file and ensure that a copy of it is attached to the entry on my file whenever you provide anyone with information included in the entry or any information based on it.

Note of correction
I, [name], of [address], would like it to be known that the County Court Judgment recorded against me for [amount] concerns a credit-card bill which I was unable to pay because I was made redundant in [month and year]. I paid the bill in full after returning to work in [month and year]. Since then, I have paid all my bills on time (as I did before losing my job) and I would ask anyone searching this file to take account of these facts.

Please confirm that the note of correction given above has been added to my file within 28 days of the date on which you receive this letter.

Yours sincerely

Name

If your note is accepted
If the agency accepts the note of correction, it must send a copy of the note to any lender that has asked for a credit reference in the six months immediately before you asked to see your file. If the note of correction relates to the judgment or decree of a court, the agency should pass your correction on so that the public records can be updated. The correction will be sent on to the other credit reference

agencies (e.g. Callcredit and Experian if you have been dealing with Equifax). If your note relates to something not held in public records, it is a good idea to check that the records of the other agency have been updated and also that lenders have been informed. Note that amendments to your file which the agency agrees to without the need for a note of correction also need to be passed on in the same way.

If your note is rejected

The agency can decide not to accept your note of correction if it thinks that the note is incorrect, defamatory, frivolous or scandalous. In such a case the agency will refer your note to the Information Commissioner for a ruling. Within 14 days of receiving the agency's request, he or she will ask for your comments. You will receive a final decision about two months later.

If you hear nothing

If you hear nothing from the agency within 28 days of it getting your letter, you can appeal to the Information Commissioner in writing giving the following details:

- your full name and address
- the name and address of the credit reference agency
- details of the entry on your file which you want corrected
- why you want the entry corrected
- why you think you will suffer if it is not corrected
- the date you sent your note of correction to the agency.

The Information Commissioner will look into your case and may ask the agency for its side of the story to help him or her make up his or her mind. If the Commissioner thinks you are right, he or she can order the agency to accept your note of correction. Whatever the Commissioner's decision, you will be informed of this after about two months.

Credit repair companies

If you are turned down for a loan due to poor credit rating, it may be tempting to use a 'credit repair company' which promises to improve your record in return for a fee. The claims made by firms of this sort are largely spurious and there is little they can do to help those in financial difficulty. Credit reference agencies such as Experian advise borrowers not to go through intermediaries but to contact the agency directly. They also provide information about credit repair on their websites.

Basic bank accounts

If you have debt problems you will almost certainly have problems with your bank as well. You may even find that the bank is one of your main creditors. If this is the case, you might want to open a new account elsewhere to prevent your income being seized before you have had a chance to meet household expenses and pay priority debts.

Although you will find it difficult to open an ordinary bank account (particularly if your creditors have taken legal action against you or you have been declared bankrupt) it is possible to opt for a 'basic bank account', which will allow you to pay in funds, set up direct debits and withdraw money from cash machines. These accounts are distinctive in that they do not permit you to go overdrawn, write cheques or obtain credit.

Most high-street banks provide basic accounts, although they tend not to promote them, concentrating instead on more profitable current accounts with credit facilities. Some banks exclude undischarged bankrupts or those convicted of fraud, although others have no restrictions of this kind. In addition to those in financial difficulty, basic bank accounts are also appropriate for people on very low incomes and those under 18.

From April 2003 most basic bank account holders will be able to draw cash at post office branches in addition to their banks. The post office will also be establishing 'card accounts' designed to receive benefits, pensions or tax credits. These are more restricted than basic accounts in that they don't accept any other kind of payment, don't allow you to pay bills by direct debit and only let you withdraw money from a post office branch.

Non-standard lenders

If you find it difficult to get credit from a bank, building society or credit-card company – because you have a poor credit rating, are on a low income or are simply over-extended – it is very tempting to resort to 'non-standard lenders', who advance money to 'high-risk' borrowers at very high rates of interest. These range from long-established licensed 'home credit' lenders to less reputable 'loan sharks', who supply unregulated door-to-door finance.

Although these lenders supply an immediate need for ready cash, they often bring problems that can seriously worsen your longer-term debt problems:

- high interest rates
- inflexible payment schedules
- high-pressure 'doorstep' agents/collectors.

A further drawback to non-standard lenders is their attitude towards borrowers who are unable to keep up repayments. Historically, they have been unwilling to accept a pro-rata share of a debtor's available income and often refuse to enter into negotiations with credit advisors, such as the Citizens Advice Bureau (CAB)★. They are also reluctant to freeze interest charges, which are so high that unpaid debts can rapidly escalate to unmanageable levels. Penalty charges for late payment (or early redemption) are also frequently imposed by non-standard lenders, irrespective of the borrower's circumstances.

Door-to door lenders are not the only creditors to charge high interest rates to 'sub-prime' customers. Car finance, kitchen sales and replacement window firms all operate finance schemes with high interest rates and restrictive conditions. Critics of this sector have referred to 'predatory lending', where those least able to afford credit end up paying most for it.

Varying rates of interest (for illustrative purposes only)	
Source of credit	Interest rate (% APR)
Typical mortgage	5–6 (or less)
Credit union	12.68 (maximum)
Bank: personal loan	6–30
Credit cards	8–20
Store cards	13-30
Catalogues	30
Home credit (door-to-door)	100
Loan sharks	500

Alternatives to non-standard lenders

As a general rule, high-interest lenders are best avoided by those in financial difficulty. Alternative loans may be available from credit unions (collective organisations which lend money to their members at low interest) or some local authorities, which provide bridging loans to those unable to borrow from mainstream lenders. For further details of credit unions contact the Association of British Credit Unions Ltd (ABCUL)★ or consult the Registry of Friendly Societies★. If you need a short-term loan to pay for essentials, such as food and clothing, you might be eligible for a Social Fund Crisis Loan from the DWP (see pages 159–63 for further details).

If you owe money to a non-standard lender and are having difficulty in making repayments you should seek financial advice from your local CAB★, Consumer Credit Counselling Service (CCCS)★ or National Debtline★.

Legal protection for borrowers

Credit agreements

There are several laws and regulations aimed at ensuring that any consumer credit agreements you sign up to are fair, and any organisations you owe money to behave reasonably.

Unfair credit agreements

Parts of the Consumer Credit Act 1974 allow a court to rewrite any credit agreement (including a mortgage) if it thinks the agreement is an 'extortionate credit bargain'. This means that it:

- has payments which are 'grossly exorbitant' (too high compared with similar agreements), or
- 'grossly contravenes the ordinary principles of fair dealing', which means you have been a victim of sharp practice.

Courts have used this law to reduce very high interest loans, especially in cases where the person signing the agreement was pressurised into signing. But this is not easy to prove, and if you think you might have a case you should get expert advice from an adviser or the trading standards department at your local council.

Unfair contract terms

When you sign a contract for credit, or to buy something, it should spell out all the terms and conditions of the deal. The law says that a company can't enforce any part of a contract if it is not in Plain English or if it is unfair (but this doesn't mean a price that you think is unfair). These regulations prevent lenders from:

- charging much higher interest to customers who have missed payments, and
- taking customers by surprise with unexpected or hidden small print or unclear wording in agreements.

If you think that there was a term in a credit agreement which you weren't aware of when you took it out, contact a legal adviser or the trading standards department at your local council.

Credit licence

Anyone who offers credit (a creditor) must have a licence from the Office of Fair Trading. Creditors who did not have a licence at the time you signed any credit agreement will not be able to legally enforce the terms of the agreement.

Most credit agreements that consumers sign are 'regulated agreements' under the Consumer Credit Act. This means that they must be in writing and also explain, among other things:

- the amount of money you are borrowing
- the interest rate, and
- how long you will be paying the debt back.

Creditors who arrange credit using regulated agreements should not be able to take court action against you if you never signed such an agreement. Creditors cannot start court action if they haven't given you an agreement to sign.

You can get advice on other details of the Consumer Credit Act from: your local CAB★ or solicitor, the Office of Fair Trading★ or the trading standards department at your local council.

Harassment

It is a criminal offence for a creditor to needlessly upset you to get you to repay.

Harassment includes:

- threatening you with a criminal prosecution when you can't be prosecuted
- pretending to be a court official
- sending letters which look like court forms, and
- telling other people, such as neighbours and your employer, about your debt to force you to pay.

If you are being harassed, keep a record of exactly what happened and when, and report it to your local trading standards department at your local council. A creditor could have its credit licence (see page 180) taken away if it is found guilty of harassing you.

If the creditor ends up taking you to court to get you to repay, you can tell the court about the harassment then. This could reduce the court costs you may have to pay. Some types of harassment may also break the Human Rights Act.

CHAPTER 11

Getting back on track

Once you have begun to tackle your debt problems, you should see a steady improvement in your financial situation. As your debts are paid off, the amount you will have to pay to creditors will fall. Eventually you should achieve a surplus, which can be put towards savings. (In essence, you will have already been doing this in order to make repayments.) You can check your progress by reusing the budget calculator introduced in Chapter 1.

Personal budget calculator	
Enter your average monthly income	A
Enter your average monthly spend on essentials	B
Subtract B from A and enter the result at C	C
The figure at C is what you have left to spend on desirables	
Enter your average monthly spend on desirables	D
Subtract D from C and enter the result at E	E

Analysing the results of your budget calculations

START

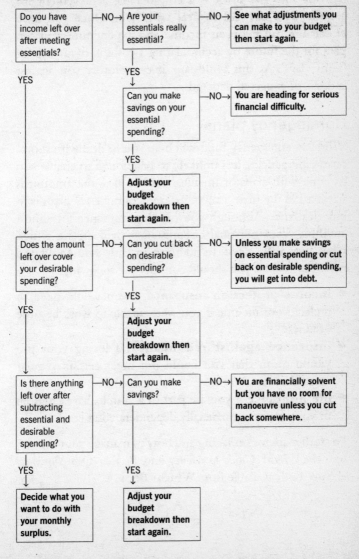

Do you have income left over after meeting essentials? —NO→ Are your essentials really essential? —NO→ **See what adjustments you can make to your budget then start again.**

YES ↓ (from "Are your essentials really essential?")

Can you make savings on your essential spending? —NO→ **You are heading for serious financial difficulty.**

YES ↓

Adjust your budget breakdown then start again.

YES (from "Do you have income left over after meeting essentials?") ↓

Does the amount left over cover your desirable spending? —NO→ Can you cut back on desirable spending? —NO→ **Unless you make savings on essential spending or cut back on desirable spending, you will get into debt.**

YES ↓ (from "Can you cut back on desirable spending?")

Adjust your budget breakdown then start again.

YES (from "Does the amount left over cover your desirable spending?") ↓

Is there anything left over after subtracting essential and desirable spending? —NO→ Can you make savings? —NO→ **You are financially solvent but you have no room for manoeuvre unless you cut back somewhere.**

YES ↓   YES ↓

Decide what you want to do with your monthly surplus.   **Adjust your budget breakdown then start again.**

Saving

Moving into the black is a considerable achievement for anyone who has had to deal with debt. Once you have closed the gap between income and expenditure, you can plan for the future by accumulating a cushion of savings for 'rainy days'. As this builds up, it can protect you against sudden, unexpected demands.

Contingency plans

While an emergency fund will help you to deal with short-term emergencies, it is unlikely to be enough to enable you to cope with a major financial crisis, unless the amount is sizeable. So the main way of making contingency plans is to buy insurance. Although you can buy insurance for almost anything, your personal circumstances will dictate which types you really need. In addition to basic household and motor insurance, you should consider the following:

- **income-protection insurance** if you would need to replace your income if you were unable to work because of illness
- **insurance against redundancy** if losing your job would mean that you could not meet certain regular monthly bills
- **life insurance** if you are part of a couple, have children or you support a financially dependent adult

For futher advice on saving and how to manage your money, see *The Which? Guide to Money* and *Be Your Own Financial Adviser*, both available from Which? Books★.

Addresses

Advice UK
12th Floor
New London Bridge House
25 London Bridge Street
London SE1 9ST
Tel: 020–7407 4070
Fax: 020–7407 4071
Email: general@adviceuk.org.uk
Website: www.adviceuk.org.uk

Age Concern
Astral House
1268 London Road
London
SW16 4ER
Information line: (0800) 009966
Website: www.ace.org.uk

Association for Payment Clearing Services (APACS)
Mercury House
Triton Court
14 Finsbury Square
London
EC2A 1LQ
Tel: 020–7711 6200
Fax: 020–7256 5527
Email: corpcomms@apacs.org.uk
Website: www.apacs.org.uk

Association of British Credit Unions Ltd
Holyoake House
Hanover Street
Manchester
M60 0AS
Tel: 0161–832 3694
Fax: 0161–832 3706
Email: info@abcul.org
Website: www.abcul.org

Association of Civil Enforcement Agencies
Chesham House
150 Regent Street
London
W1R 5FA
Tel: 020–7432 0366
Fax: 020–7432 0516
Email: sec@acea.org.uk
Website: www.acea.org.uk

British Bankers' Association
Publication Unit
Pinners Hall
105–108 Old Broad Street
London EC2A 1EX
Tel: 020–7216 8816
Fax: 020–7216 8920
Email: publications@bba.org.uk
Website: www.bba.org.uk

Building Societies' Association
3 Savile Row
London
W1S 3PB
Tel: 020–7437 0655
Fax: 020–7734 6416
Website: www.bsa.org.uk

Business Debtline
Tel: (0800) 197 6026
Website: www.bdl.org.uk

Callcredit plc
Consumer Services Team
PO Box 491
Leeds
LS3 1WZ
Tel: 0870 060 1414
Email: info@callcredit.plc.uk
Website: www.callcredit.plc.uk

Child Poverty Action Group
94 White Lion Street
London
N1 9PF
Tel: 020–7837 7979
Email: book.orders@cpag.demon.co.uk
Website: www.cpag.org.uk

Child Support Agency (CSA)
PO Box 55, Brierley Hill, West Midlands
DY5 1YL
Tel: (0845) 713 3133 (local rate)
Minicom: (0845) 713 8924
Fax: 0151–649 2095
E-mail: csa-nel@dwp.gsi.gov.uk
Website: www.csa.gov.uk

Citizens' Advice Bureaux
Look in The Phone Book under 'Citizens'
Advice Bureau'.
Websites:
www.nacab.org.uk
www.adviceguide.org.uk

Consumer Credit Counselling Service
Wade House
Merrion Centre
Leeds LS2 8NG
Tel: (0800) 138 1111
Fax: 0113–297 0101
Email: info@cccs.co.uk
Website: www.cccs.co.uk

Council of Mortgage Lenders
3 Savile Row
London
W1S 3PB
Tel: 020–7437 0075
Fax: 020–7437 3791
Email: info@cml.org.uk
Website: www.cml.org.uk

Credit Services Association Ltd
3 Albany Mews
Montagu Avenue
Newcastle upon Tyne
NE3 4JW
Tel: 0191–213 2509
Fax: 0191–284 5431
Email: mail@csa-uk.com
Website: www.csa-uk.com

Department of Education for Northern Ireland
Rathgael House
43 Balloo Road
Bangor
County Down
BT19 7PR
Tel: 028–9127 9279
Fax: 028–9127 9100
Email: mail@deni.gov.uk
Website: www.deni.gov.uk

Department for Education and Skills (DfES)
Public Enquiry Unit
PO Box 12
Runcorn
Cheshire
WA7 2GJ
Tel: (0870) 000 2288
Fax: (01928) 794248
Email: info@dfes.gsi.gov.uk
Website: www.dfes.gov.uk

Department for Work and Pensions
Correspondence Unit
Room 540
The Adelphi
1–11 John Adam Street
London WC2N 6HT
Tel: 020–7712 2171
DWP Benefit Enquiry Line: (0800) 882200
Direct Payment Enquiry Line: (0800) 107 2000
Fax: 020–7712 2386
Email: peo@dwp.gsi.gov.uk
Websites: www.dwp.gov.uk
www.jobcentreplus.gov.uk

Disability Law Service
39–45 Cavell Street
London
E1 2BP
Tel: 020–7791 9800
Fax: 020–7791 9802
Email: advice@dls.org.uk

DIAL UK
St Catherine's
Tickhill Road
Doncaster
DN4 8QN
Tel: (01302) 310123
Fax: (01302) 310404
Email: enquiries@dialuk.org.uk
Website: www.dialuk.org.uk

Energywatch
Head Office
4th Floor
Artillery House
Artillery Row
London SW1P 1RT
Tel: (0845) 906 0708 (gas)
(0845) 601 3131 (electricity)
Fax: 020–7799 8341
Email: enquiries@energywatch.org.uk
Website: www.energywatch.org.uk

Enforcement Services Association
Ridgefield House
14 John Dalton Street
Manchester
M2 6JR
Tel: 0161 839 7225
Fax: 0161 834 2433
Email: director@bailiffs.org.uk
Website: www.bailiffs.org.uk

Equifax plc
Credit File Advice Centre
PO Box 1140
Bradford
BD1 5US
Tel: 0870 010 0583
Email: contactcis.uk@equifax.com
Website: www.equifax.co.uk

Experian Ltd
Consumer Help Service
PO Box 8000
Nottingham
NG1 5GX
Tel: 0870 241 6212
Email: experian_consumerhelp@experian-
mail.custhelp.com
Website: www.experian.co.uk

Finance and Leasing Association
2nd Floor
Imperial House
15–19 Kingsway
London WC2B 6UN
Tel: 020–7836 6511
Fax: 020–7420 9600
Email: info@fla.org.uk
Website: www.fla.org.uk

Financial Ombudsman Service
South Quay Plaza
183 Marsh Wall
London E14 9SR
Tel: (0845) 080 1800
020–7964 1000 (for calls from outside the
UK)
Fax: 020–7964 1001
Email: enquiries@financial-
ombudsman.org.uk
Website: www.financial-ombudsman.org.uk

HM Customs and Excise
Tel: (0845) 010 9000
Website: www.hmce.gov.uk

HM Land Registry
32 Lincoln's Inn Fields
London WC2A 3PH
Tel: 020–7917 8888
Fax: 020–7955 0110
Website: www.landreg.gov.uk

HM Treasury
Public Enquiry Unit
1 Horse Guards Road
London
SW1A 2HQ
Tel: 020–7270 4558
Fax: 020–7270 4574
Email: public.enquiries@hm-treasury.gsi.
gov.uk
Website: www.hm-treasury.gov.uk

IFA Promotions Office
17–19 Emery Road
Brislington
Bristol
BS4 5PF
Tel: 0800 085 3250
Website: www.unbiased.co.uk

Information Commissioner
Wycliffe House
Water Lane
Wilmslow
Cheshire
SK9 5AF
Tel: (01625) 545745
Fax: (01625) 524510
Email: data@dataprotection.gov.uk
Website: www.dataprotection.gov.uk

Inland Revenue
For local tax enquiry centres look in The
Phone Book under 'Inland Revenue'
    For your own tax office, check your tax
return, other tax correspondence or check
with your employer or scheme paying you a
pension.
Website: www.inlandrevenue.gov.uk
General enquiry line: 020–7667 4001
To get Inland Revenue leaflets, phone the
Orderline: 0845 900 0404 (minicom
available on this number)
Fax: 0845 900 0604
Email: saorderline.ir@gtnet.gov.uk
Inland Revenue Self-employment Helpline:
0845 915 4515

The Insolvency Service
21 Bloomsbury Street
London WC1B 3QW
Central public enquiry line: 020–7291 6895
Fax: 020–7636 4709
Website: www.insolvency.gov.uk

Law Centres Federation
Duchess House
18–19 Warren Street
London
W1T 5LR
Tel: 020–7387 8570
Email: info@lawcentres.org.uk
Website: www.lawcentres.org.uk

Lord Chancellor's Department
Selborne House
54–60 Victoria Street
London
SW1E 6QW
Tel: 020–7210 8500
Email: general.queries@lcdhg.gsi.gov.uk
Website: www.lcd.gov.uk

The Mail Order Traders Association
PO Box 1023
Liverpool
L69 2WS
Tel: 0151–227 9456
Fax: 0151–227 9678
Email: k.doust@mota.uk.com
Website: www.emota-aevpc.org

Money Advice Association
Kempton House
Dysart Road
Grantham
NG31 7LE
Tel: (01476) 594970
Fax: (01476) 591204
Email: office@m-a-a.org.uk
Website: www.m-a-a.org.uk

Money Advice Trust
Bridge House
181 Queen Victoria Street
London EC4V 4DZ
Tel: 020–7489 7796
Fax: 020–7489 7704
Email: info@moneyadvicetrust.org
Website: www.moneyadvicetrust.org

National Consumer Credit Federation
98–100 Holme Lane
Sheffield
S6
Tel/Fax: 0114–234 8101
Email: nccf alk21.com

National Debtline
The Arch
48–52 Floodgate Street
Birmingham
B5 5SL
Tel: (0808) 808 4000 (freephone)
Fax: 0121–703 6940
Website: www.nationaldebtline.co.uk

Office of Fair Trading (OFT)
Fleetbank House
2–6 Salisbury Square
London
EC4Y 8JX
Tel: (0845) 722 4499 *local rate*
Fax: 020–7211 8877
Email: enquiries@oft.gsi.gov.uk
Website: www.oft.gov.uk

Office of Gas and Electricity Markets (OFGEM)
9 Millbank
London SW1P 3GE
Tel: 020–7901 7000
Fax: 020–7901 7066
Website: www.ofgem.gov.uk
or:
Regents Court
70 West Regent Street
Glasgow G2 2QZ
Tel: 0141–331 2678
Fax: 0141–331 2777
Website: as above

OFTEL
50 Ludgate Hill
London
EC4M 7JJ
Tel: 020–7634 8700
Fax: 020–7634 8943
Email: infocent.oftel@gtnet.gov.uk
Website: www.oftel.gov.uk

The Official Receiver
Public Enquiry Unit
PO Box 203
21 Bloomsbury Street
London WC1B 3SS
Central public enquiry line: 020–7291 6895
Fax: 020–7636 4709
Website: www.insolvency.gov.uk

Payplan
Kempton House
Dysart Road
Grantham
NG31 7LE
Tel: 0800 085 4298
Email: help@payplan.com
Website: www.payplan.com

Post Office
Tel: (0845) 722 3344
Website: www.royalmail.com
For enquiries on an established Direct Payment Card Account

Student Awards Agency for Scotland
Gyleview House
3 Redheughs Rigg
Edinburgh
EH12 9HH
Tel: 0131–476 8212
Email: saas.geu@scotland.gsi.gov.uk
Website: www.student-support-saas.gov.uk

Student Loans Company Ltd
100 Bothwell Street
Glasgow
G2 7JD
Tel: 0141–306 2000
(0870) 242 2211
Fax: 0141–306 2005
Website: www.slc.co.uk

TaxAid
Room 304
Linton House
164–180 Union Street
Southwark
London SE1 0LH
Helpline: 020–7803 4959 Mon–Thurs
10am–12pm
Email: contact axaid.org.uk
Website: www.taxaid.org.uk

Which? Books
PO Box 44
Hertford X
SG14 1LH
Tel: (0800) 252100
Fax: (0800) 533053
Website: www.which.net

Youth Access
2 Taylors Yard
67 Alderbrook Road
Clapham
SW12 8AD
Tel: 020–8772 9900
Fax: 020–8772 9746
Email: admin@youthaccess.org.uk

Index